Nov. 3, 2015

LiViNG
the Resurrection

REFLECTIONS AFTER EASTER

To Jan
With affection

C. FRANKLIN BROOKHART

+C. Franklin Brookhart

MP | More
NEW YO

I0980881

To the clergy and people of the Diocese of Montana,

and to my wife Susan,

I dedicate this book, praying that it will glorify the Risen Christ.

Morehouse Publishing, 4775 Linglestown Road, Harrisburg, PA 17112

Morehouse Publishing, 445 Fifth Avenue, New York, NY 10016

Morehouse Publishing is an imprint of Church Publishing Incorporated.
www.churchpublishing.org

Cover design by Laurie Klein Westhafer

Typeset by Rose Design

Library of Congress Cataloging-in-Publication Data

A catalog record for this book is available from the Library of Congress

ISBN-13: 978-0-8192-2795-9 (pbk.)

ISBN-13: 978-0-8192-2796-6 (ebook)

Printed in the United States of America

Contents

Acknowledgments

For me, gratitude is one of the gifts of living the resurrection. So it would be a grievous lack of integrity on my part if I did not acknowledge and thank many people for their support in this writing project. I am grateful to God for what they have given me.

Two years ago the Standing Committee of the Diocese of Montana began to urge me to take a sabbatical leave. I had never had one, and was both a little fearful and a bit daunted by the prospect of three months away from my responsibilities. But they insisted that I had a duty to model good stewardship of my job, and I relented. I am grateful to them for their foresight and good sense.

As part of my sabbatical time, I asked and received permission to be present for a week as Bishop-in-Residence at The School of Theology, The University of the South, Sewanee, Tennessee. The dean and president, the Very Rev. Dr. William S. Stafford, made that possible and welcomed me warmly. I spent most of my time in the seminary's superb theological library, and was there helped in significant ways by Dr. James Warren Dunkly, School of Theology Librarian. Also, the Rev. Dr. Christopher Bryan, C. K. Benedict professor of New Testament, allowed me to tap into his extensive knowledge of and wisdom about the resurrection. To them I am grateful.

Later the Seminary of the Southwest, Austin, Texas, opened its facilities to me for two weeks. The school's theological collection is also superb, and I was guided and assisted by Dr. Donald E. Keeny, director of the Booher Library, and his staff. And the welcome and encouragement of the dean and president, the Very Rev. Douglas Travis, could hardly have been warmer. My gratitude overflows for their help.

Along the way I was assisted in important ways by the Rev. Canon C.K. Robertson, canon to the Presiding Bishop and Primate. I salute him and thank him. Nancy Bryan of Church Publishing, Inc. edited my work, and I appreciate her comments and guidance, which made my work better.

Introduction

After reading even a little of the writing of St. Paul in the New Testament, the accusation could not be made that Paul did not know what he believed or was reluctant to state it. Some of his most powerful and compelling material can be found in 1 Corinthians 15, where he tackles the elusive category of resurrection. He states, "If Christ has not been raised, then our proclamation has been in vain and your faith has been in vain" (verse 14). Then he sharpens his point, "If Christ has not been raised, your faith is futile and you are still in your sins" (verse 17).

Clear enough? Paul asserts that the resurrection of Jesus Christ from the dead forms the foundation of the Good News, and, therefore, of the life of the church.

Since "resurrection" is not a word that we throw around in daily conversation, we need to set out some guidelines for our use of this word. "Resurrection" declares that on the third day after his death on the cross, on that first Easter morning, Jesus was raised from the dead by the power of God in such a way that he now lives forever beyond the power of death and of all else that separates humanity from God. Paul again has an eloquent definition: "We know that Christ, being raised from the dead, will never die again; death no longer has dominion over him" (Romans 6:9). We are speaking of a great mystery that, if true, would radically transform the way we live and think.

Consider that the New Testament is as studded with references to the resurrection of Jesus as the night sky is studded with stars. Further, the early Christians were firm in their belief, from a certain perspective, that the Old Testament, too, points toward Easter. Furthermore, the ecumenical creeds, the liturgy, the hymns of the church are shot through with resurrection and Easter references. In summary all the foundational and authoritative resources of the Christian religion lift up the stunning act of God raising Jesus Christ from the dead on Easter.

So, to ponder the resurrection is to stand at the very heart of the Christian faith. Nevertheless, three difficulties nag at us as we consider the events of Easter. First, the concept of resurrection cannot be easily grasped; there are no other events to compare with it or to serve as analogs.

Second, we tend to bring twenty-first century skepticism with us. We believe that the dead stay dead, and cannot explain how such an event as the resurrection might happen. I hope the following chapters will help us step up to dealing with these doubts.

The third issue is the one I wish to explore in some detail. The question is: How do we live the resurrection? Or, to use New Testament imagery, how do we conduct our lives as part of the new creation and share in the abundant life Jesus promised? These questions have been much on my mind as I have the privilege of serving the Risen Lord as bishop among the clergy and people of Montana. I have understood my call in the words of the liturgy for the ordination of a bishop in *The Book of Common Prayer*: "A bishop in God's holy Church is called to be one with the apostles in proclaiming Christ's resurrection and interpreting the Gospel" (p. 517). My basic vision for the church is a resurrectional one: a community itself transformed and then transforming the world by the power of the Resurrected Lord. This book is my attempt to work on these three issues, so that lives of individuals, of churches, of dioceses are transformed by the active presence of the Risen One, so that all we say and do gives witness to resurrection.

I have had a lifelong fascination with railroading. One of the most vivid memories of childhood was a trip with my grandparents on B & O's National Limited, one of those classic luxury passenger trains of the last century. We climbed up into the train, sat in the plush seats, and watched the world race by. We walked the length of the train, ate apple pie in the dining car, and finally stepped out onto the platform in a new place. That was when I first began to understand the concept of travel and journey: you start here, and end there.

I hope we can start where we are as human beings and end in a new place with a deeper and more joyful sense of living in the resurrection reality.

chapter 1

It Begins in the Garden

In the gospel according to John, we are told that Jesus was buried in a tomb, which was located in a garden near the place of his crucifixion. On Easter morning Mary Magdalene goes to the garden, is shocked to find that the massive stone covering the entry to the tomb had been rolled away, and that the body of Jesus is no longer there. Her initial interpretation of the situation is that someone had stolen the body—sensible and logical reasoning, it seems to me. While there, the Risen Lord encounters Mary, but she does not recognize him and assumes that he is the gardener. This is where we begin, in a garden, and as you see, that garden is an ambiguous place, a place with associations of both death and life.

We, however, need to begin at the beginning.

John's horticultural setting harkens back to another garden found in the second chapter of the first book of scripture, Genesis, and it, too, is a place of ambiguity. This scriptural passage narrates the story of God creating a garden, which God then populates with plants, trees, animals, and eventually two human beings who are called simply the man and the woman. I think we will largely miss the point of this episode if we try to deal with it as if it were a report of an event from the front page of the paper. As we will see, there are elements in the story that tip us off that, rather than an account of a specific event in time and space, we are instead dealing with a timeless story about the relationship between God and humanity. It is a story filled with truth, and, if we read it carefully, we will find a place for ourselves in it.

To begin, we find God playing in the dirt. He shapes a human form out of soil, then leans over and breathes into the nostrils, and the man ("adam" in the original language) becomes a living being. Up until then the world was a barren place with no fauna or flora; there was no rainfall, and it was watered by a single spring. Next, God creates a garden paradise filled with plants and trees, rivers and minerals. These things evoke in the man a sense of wonder at their beauty, and they provide food for him. The man is placed in the midst of the garden, which is located somewhere to the east of a place called Eden.

At this point we come to a significant detail in the story. In the middle of the garden, God has planted the tree of life and the tree of the knowledge of good and evil. These are plants found in no field guide, and this is an orchard like none we have ever seen. Our intuition tells us that trouble is ahead, if for no other reason than that issues of right and wrong and of life have always challenged the best minds and most well-intentioned hearts in history.

God gives the man a job: he is to tend the garden. But there is a cautionary comment to the man: you may eat as much as you want of the fruit of any of the trees, but do not—I repeat—do not eat of the tree of life or of the tree of the knowledge of good and evil. They are off-limits to the man—too morally and intellectually hot to handle.

The story then takes a turn. God announces that it is not a good thing for the man to be alone in this amazing place. So, God creates the animals and trots them before the man, who gives them names, a sign that God values the role and place of the man. In the ancient near east, the privilege of bestowing names was a great honor and responsibility, because a name hinted at the essence of that being. But neither God nor the man seem satisfied with developments thus far, so God puts the man to sleep and performs a rib-ectomy. God then uses the rib to make a woman. God awakens the man and shows him the latest bit of creation. In reaction to the sight of the woman, the man says, "Wow! You got it right this time, God!"

Who could imagine a more moving and beautiful story? Everything is, shall we say, perfect. The man and woman have the significant job of tending to the garden, which in turn gives the pair food. Every day in the afternoon—and apparently every day is a warm summer day—the man and woman take a stroll with their Creator. The world, humanity, and God all live in perfect concord.

But the story seems like a dream to us, does it not? We can imagine it, dream about it, long for it, and even see some of the continuities with our own situation, but this is not our world. Concord and harmony are not words we would use as adjectives for our situation. Our world is no paradise.

Soon a kind of darkness descends over the story and the paradise garden. The man and woman find themselves under the tree of the knowledge of good and evil. A crafty creature, the serpent, appears and tells the couple to enjoy the fruit of that special tree. "Oh, no," the woman says. "God has told us we will die if we do." The serpent says, "That's baloney. If you do eat, you will understand the difference between good and evil, and then you will be like God." This is simply too much for the two to handle, and they help themselves to the fruit of the tree. Until now, they had known only God and the good, but now. . . .

The story underscores the new situation of the woman and the man in simple and striking detail. The two eat the fruit and suddenly realize that things are not right, that they are naked. Now shame, guilt, and fear have entered the picture, and the garden does not seem like paradise anymore.

At the time of the daily afternoon stroll, God cannot find the two, because they are hiding. God asks a question filled with implications: where are you? They step out, and admit that they had hidden themselves in fear, knowing they were naked and vulnerable before God. The Creator knows something is terribly wrong, and asks, "Who told you that you were naked?"

In the tense conversation that follows, the woman and man try to blame each other for listening to the serpent and eating the fruit. At that point, God does not point a finger of judgment at them, but rather describes what they will experience now that they can discern good from evil. The man will have to work hard all his life to grow food, but the soil will now produce weeds and thistles, and then in the end the man will die and return to the dust from whence he came. The woman's situation will be no better. She will have pain in childbearing and yet she will still be inextricably drawn to her husband, who will seek to dominate her. And the story ends on a very poignant note: God sends the couple out of the garden to which they will never return.

If we are honest with ourselves, we have to admit that this second part of the story is strangely familiar. Like the man and the woman, we are able to recognize beauty, justice, truth, and love, and we have a sense that we have been made by a loving Creator. And, like the man and woman, we seem to be always walking away from these things. We create some beauty, but also lots of ugliness. We desire justice, but never seem to get it entirely right. We are motivated to receive love, but find it hard to give love. And then there's God. Would it be fair to say that our relationship with the Creator is tense? Do we not, in one way or another, try to hide from the Divine?

Thus, our lives are filled with regret, fear, shame, and unfulfilled longings. We live with the nearly unbearable tension between good and evil. We try to set up our little world so that we can be a tiny god in control of that world, but we never succeed with this plan. We seek escape in buying and selling, traveling and looking, playing and frolicking. But then, like the conclusion of a cruel joke, we die. From dust we come, and to dust we return.

We live our lives outside the garden in a world of pain and perplexity. We try to find a way back to paradise, but our search is always futile. We don't know the way back and cannot find the entrance. We seek the way in success, power, influence, learning, recreation, wealth, and dozens of other things, but we forever find ourselves lost somewhere outside the garden.

It begins in a life-giving garden. We live outside that garden. We understand that it has become a place of death. But, note well, that is not the end of the story. God has made plans.

Questions to Help You Understand this Chapter's Full Intent

1. What does this creation story say about God?
2. In this story God does not intervene to prevent the man and woman from eating the fruit of the tree of knowledge of good and evil. What might this say about the pattern of God's actions toward humanity?
3. In what ways do you see yourself, your family, your church in this story?
4. In what ways does the story both comfort and challenge you?

chapter 2

It's a Scary World Out There

I imagine this scene. On a spring morning you are chatting with a friend about the Easter celebration at her church on the previous Sunday. She tells a strange story. "When the gospel story about the resurrection of Jesus was read, I became weak and felt faint. It filled me with such fear that I had to leave." You would likely ask yourself, "What kind of church is that anyway? Did she confuse church with a scary movie?"

We find it difficult to imagine such a scene. But, in fact, Easter forces us to face the issue of our fear head-on. Easter addresses that scary world out there, the world we inhabit.

Here is the Easter story as it is recorded in the gospel according to Mark:

> When the sabbath was over, Mary Magdalene, and Mary the mother of James, and Salome bought spices, so that they might go and anoint him. And very early on the first day of the week, when the sun had risen, they went to the tomb. They had been saying to one another, "Who will roll away the stone for us from the entrance to the tomb?" When they looked up, they saw that the stone, which was very large, had already been rolled back. As they entered the tomb, they saw a young man, dressed in a white robe, sitting on the right side; and they were alarmed. But he said

7

to them, "Do not be alarmed; you are looking for Jesus of Naza-
reth, who was crucified. He has been raised; he is not here. Look,
there is the place they laid him. But go, tell his disciples and Peter
that he is going ahead of you to Galilee; there you will see him,
just as he told you." So they went out and fled from the tomb, for
terror and amazement had seized them; and they said nothing to
anyone, for they were afraid. (Mark 16:1–8)

Most scholars today are convinced that this is the genuine
ending of Mark's gospel as the evangelist intended it. If that is so
(and the case is convincing), then the story contains no account
of an encounter with the Risen Christ, and the last phrase in the
narrative is "they were afraid." The emotional state of the three
women at the tomb is described in these four terms: alarm, terror,
amazement, and fear.

This is clearly not the Easter we are accustomed to in our
churches. We expect the perfume of lilies; joyous alleluias; the
music of choirs, organs, and trumpets; and the best vestments
and communion vessels. For most of us, there is no more upbeat,
exhilarating Sunday than Easter.

What are we to make, then, of Mark's narrative? I think that
this account asks us to wrestle with another side of the resurrection. This is a story with no joy and apparently no meeting with
the Risen One. The New Jerusalem Bible captures the emotional
tone with this translation: "They were frightened out of their
wits . . . they were afraid." This gospel account asks us to wrestle with the issue of fear. With apologies to Simon and Garfunkel,
this narrative asks us to sing, "Hello fear, my old friend."

I admit that this Marcan account of the resurrection has
always left me personally unsettled. And I find it a nightmare to

try to base a sermon on this particular passage. I hardly know how to react to it and what to make of it. But it is the very strangeness of the thing that forces me to pursue the meaning of the story. My own spiritual experience has led me to see that often the most difficult biblical stories are likely to be the ones that God most wants me to struggle with.

So, let's set aside our own emotional reactions and puzzlement and dive into this unsettling account. Let's look at those four terms used to describe the women's response. First is alarm. Since the New Testament was written in Greek, we can turn to a Greek lexicon to try to capture the nuances of this word. Looking at the various possible meanings and citations, the lexicon suggests that alarm here means utter astonishment so intense that one is forced to rethink ordinary assumptions.

The women also, we are told, experienced terror. That term suggests an event so out of the norm that it induces fear and even physical trembling. The three were so stunned and shaken by the empty tomb and the message of the angelic young man that their hands shook and their knees trembled.

The word amazement suggests a similar reaction. The Greek term points to a state of being so distressed that one is overwhelmed. We might say that the emotional circuits of the three women were burned out.

Finally, there is nothing fancy about the last of this quartet of terms, namely, fear. It is plain old apprehension. It is that state of mind in which a rush of adrenaline sets off one's "flight or fight" response. And, indeed, we are told that they took flight.

Part of the value of this word-study lies in its ability to raise to our awareness just how much fear and apprehension dominate our lives. We have no problem recognizing the responses of the three women. I can confess that I am an expert on anxiety and that I could teach graduate classes in worry. What about you?

I believe that fear is not an entity unto itself, but is really a symptom of other factors at work at a deep and foundational level of our lives. Please allow me to take a stab at dissecting fear into its component parts. As I have thought and read about the workings of fear—and I have done so exactly because I do not like the way fear dominates my life—I have found it helpful to think of fear as a signal, one that we need to address a cluster of four factors that are at work in the deep basement of our lives.

- Out of our past comes guilt. We carry with us a burden of shame, regret, and culpability, and the list of the particulars can be quite long. As the confession in *The Book of Common Prayer* puts it so eloquently, we are guilty by virtue of "thought, word, and deed, by what we have done, and by what we have left undone." It is at that point that fear enters. What if these things were exposed and made public? What if people found out who I really am? If people really knew me, would they not step back from a close relationship? How can I put up a good, respectable front? How can I guard my secret self?

- In the present we are plagued by the question of purpose. We have a life well stocked with gifts, interests, and talents. How do we harness these so that we live well? How can we live in such a way as to make the world a better place? It is just at that point that fear begins its whisperings in our mind. Maybe there is no meaning or purpose to life. Perhaps I am just a tiny, insignificant cog in a huge, impersonal machine. Is it possible that I have missed the important turning points in my life and am now just lost in the woods?

- The future poses the problem of death. For example, one of the most solemn days of the year for Christians is Ash Wednesday. The palms from the previous year's celebration of Palm Sunday have been burned and reduced to ash in preparation for their imposition on the foreheads of those who present themselves. I experience the act as a liturgical ordeal. The priest says, "Remember that you are dust, and to dust you shall return." The sign of Easter victory, the palms, have been turned into the mark of death. Who can leave without being shaken? Put baldly, we fear death.

- Finally, and perhaps most importantly, we have an overarching and lifelong ache at the very center of our lives. We all want to be known and valued. We want to be accepted and told that we are significant. We want to be listened to. And we want all of these on a dependable and trustworthy basis. In short, we want and need to be loved. I believe this may well be the deepest need of every human person. But exactly because this is so important, fear acts in and through that need in its more virulent forms. What if I am unlovable? What if love fails? What if I give myself to a beloved, but the gift of my love is rejected? What if I am loved in a fleeting and undependable way? If any of the above were to happen, would I not be devastated at the core of existence? Because we want and need love so much, it can be, therefore, the source of our greatest fears.

We can say, then, that fear works in complicated ways in human life. But it is also a powerful factor in the lives of congregations. As a bishop in the church, I must meet with priestly and lay leaders of parishes for a variety of reasons, such as episcopal visitations or meetings with congregations searching for a new priest. In nearly every one of those events, someone will ask a question that reveals the fears of that parish. For instance, why do we exist and what is our purpose? Why are we so burdened with tales of woe and pain from the past? Are we as a church in a spiral of decline and on our way to death? How can we stop fighting with each other? Why are outsiders not attracted to us? Your congregation, too, likely has its unique litany of fears.

This has been a bit of a detour into the structures of fear and anxiety. I, however, believe that it is important for us to start to appreciate both the extent and depth of fear at work in our lives and churches. Or to put it another way, we need to recognize how much of our lives are spent like the three women at the tomb.

For many years I spent a week every summer at our diocesan church camp located in the beautiful Appalachian Mountains. During free time I would sometimes wander through the hills surrounding the camp itself. I often found my way to a little cemetery, so hidden away in the woods that most people did not know it was there. During my first visit I noted the odd fact that many of the gravestones said that the interred persons had died in 1918 and that many were children. I then recalled that 1918 was the year of the great influenza pandemic that swept the world and killed thousands. All of those people in that tiny cemetery had died of the flu. It seemed odd that such an ordinary and common disease could cause worldwide death and pain. Fear is flu of the inner life. It touches all, everywhere. It causes death.

Given all of this, we are ready to look again at the account of the first Easter from Mark's gospel. Remember the three women caught in fear and trembling—and rightly so. If the message of the angelic young man was true and taken seriously, then everything about life as they knew and understood it had to undergo a basic and foundational change. They knew, as do we, that dead people stay dead, that all things pass away, that mortality is *the* fact of life, that death always has the last word. Moreover, these are the women who had accompanied Jesus throughout his ministry, and as one of the other gospels tells us, they financially supported Jesus' work (Matt. 27:55). They had seen him push the boundaries of their understanding when he cured the incurable and cast out demons. No prophet had delivered a word from God for over three hundred years, and here was Jesus insisting that the rule of God had begun. I am certain that they had begun to understand that God was close at hand in the person and work of Jesus; he was a walking mystery, but they sensed in him divine truth in action. In my imagination I see them saying to each other, "To be in the presence of Jesus is to be in the presence of God." Jesus had taken their minds and hearts, their imaginations and wills to places they had never believed possible.

But it all came to a lurching end in just a matter of a few days. Jesus was betrayed by a member of his inner circle, he was condemned by a kangaroo court, deserted by his friends, and sentenced to die a painful and ignominious death. For Jesus' followers, the bottom had dropped out of their hopes and dreams, out of their prayers and longings.

In the tradition of the Eastern Church, there are two icons for Easter. One is called the "Myrrhbearers," and it shows the women of the gospel stories arriving at the tomb. They have wrapped themselves in their cloaks so that only part of each of their faces is visible, and they each carry a little jar of myrrh to anoint Jesus' body. Wrapped up in fear, carrying around symbols of death and decay—that is where they were that morning, and that is where we dwell, too.

But with the angelic announcement and the sight of the empty tomb, the three begin to perceive that Jesus was not just pushing the boundaries, but had, in the resurrection, shattered the boundaries of their minds and imaginations. Those early followers of Jesus were transformed by the resurrection. Their old lives were shattered. Their old understandings were rendered useless and their fear void. All of the anxiety of the three was focused and powerful as they approached the tomb of Jesus. But what happened after the initial shock of the young man's announcement and the sight of the vacant tomb was the beginning of what St. Paul would later call the new creation.

At this point of heightened fear, the women would soon be stunned into three, great, overwhelming, life-transforming, paradigm-shifting understandings. First, they sensed that God had acted in the mightiest of ways in the resurrection. It was God who had raised Jesus from the dead. In much of the New Testament, the resurrection is rendered in the passive mode: "Christ was raised," not "Christ rose." The use of the passive indicates that it is God who acted decisively in regard to Jesus. It is St. Paul again who offers this poetic and succinct definition of Easter morning: "Christ, being raised from the dead, will never die again; death no longer has dominion over him" (Romans 6:9).

Second, in the resurrection God put a seal of approval on all that Jesus had said and done, and especially on his suffering and death. In the United States we are familiar with the Good Housekeeping Seal of Approval. The appearance of the familiar little oval and the above words on a product says to us, "We have tested and tried what you are about to buy, and it is the real thing." The resurrection is God's guarantee that in Jesus the rule of God was close enough to touch, that Jesus' ministry was God's ministry.

Third, the resurrection proclaims that life and love will always prevail when God is at work. Guilt, aimlessness, death, rejection, and fear never win in the end. If God can deal with death, God can deal with anything.

If we were to meet in person, you would very likely also meet my nearly constant companion Lizzie, my English springer spaniel. When she was a puppy, her favorite game was tug: I would hold one end of a rope in my hands and she would hold the other in her mouth. The growling and shaking of her head were signs of her determination to win. Her veterinarian chided me about the game: "You can play tug, but never let her win, because then she will think she is in charge." The resurrection demonstrates who is in charge and who the victor is.

Little wonder early Christians were transformed. Little wonder that they were able to see and become part of the dawning of God's new creation.

Please note very carefully the first words of the angelic messenger to the three women: "Do not be alarmed." There it is! One of the great implications of the resurrection is contained in those words. Do not be alarmed. Do not be afraid, terrified, scared. To live in the resurrection is to cease to be dominated by fear. The women in Mark's narrative did not understand, because they fled in fear. But clearly that was not the end of the story for them, otherwise we would never have heard about the events of Easter. The day would come when they could both hear and believe the words of the messenger.

The great motivator of our lives need not be fear, worry, or anxiety. The resurrection announces to us that God can deal with all of those factors that push us into fear. Let me hasten to add that there are legitimate reasons to have fear. I am afraid, for example, that I could wreck my truck and die on an icy road. But to have fear is not the same thing as to live in fear. The resurrection frees us from that.

One of the historic aspects of Easter is as the supreme time for baptisms. This practice goes back to our earliest records about the life of the church. It is no accident that Easter and baptism are so intertwined theologically and liturgically. In the sacramental act of baptism, God is actually acting and doing something to and for us. In baptism, we are promised that we are joined to the death and resurrection of the Risen Christ. To be baptized into Christ means that Jesus' story will be our story, that God will act in and for us so as to bring love out of rejection, forgiveness out of guilt, purpose out of aimlessness, and life out of death. This movement from the cross to the empty tomb, from death to life, from the dying to the raising of our Lord, is called the Paschal Mystery. In ways beyond our imagining and understanding, God has promised that God will do for us what God did for Jesus.

What if we could take the resurrection, chew it, swallow it, and make it a part of ourselves? Incidentally, is that not what we do when we receive the presence of the Risen Lord in the Holy Eucharist? What if we could internalize resurrection in just the way we internalize the bread and wine, the Body and Blood of the Risen One? What would happen to us as persons and as a church if we stepped out of the tomb and into the new reality of resurrection?

I suggest that we take three steps that will help us to that end. First, learn to be aware of the fears in your life and church, and explore what it is that you are afraid of and why. One of the basics of weight loss is to learn to be aware of our hunger, of when and why we eat. In a similar way the Marcan narrative of the resurrection can cause us to become aware of fear and to explore its nature. The first step toward resurrection for the three women was to recognize the fear. Remember they ask themselves, "Who will roll away the stone?" How will we cope with that big rock? And we ask ourselves, how will we cope with rocky roads and stone-hard barriers and the hard pain that blocks our lives? Be aware of the worry and anxiety.

Second, have the courage to name it, even if you only do so in the quiet of your mind. By saying "I am now afraid," we are on our way toward the resurrection life. I once served a church at which parish meetings always seemed to have a contentious and angry edge. One of the most valuable members of that congregation had the gift of being able to wait until just the right moment in the debate, and then he would stand and with a smile accurately name what we were afraid of as a church. Over time those meetings provoked less and less fear in me when I began to trust that Lou would do his resurrection thing. His naming the fear was like rolling away the stone. My wife and I would later discuss those meetings, and she would say, "You can always trust Lou." That period of time was when I began to live into the resurrection more fully, to trust God.

Third, carry as a mantra the words of the angelic young man, "Do not be afraid." If you want to make use of some free time, get a hold of a concordance to the Bible and look up the word "afraid."

What you will learn is that that phrase "Do not be afraid" or some variant of it constitutes one of the great, overarching themes of the Bible. That is good warrant for making those four words a constant and conscious part of our lives as persons and churches.

One of the interesting aspects of living in Montana is the large parts of the state considered free range for cattle and horses. Signs along the road warn when you are entering one of these areas, and it is the driver's responsibility to watch for the livestock that sometimes inhabit the road. There are places, however, where you do not want cattle to roam. Entrances to ranches and farms, and ramps onto the highways are examples. At those places people install a metal or wooden grate across the road, and they make sure there is an open space under the grate. These devices are called cattle guards. For some reason horses and cows will not walk on a surface that they can see through. My guess is that at some level of instinct, they do not trust that the grate will support them. I can imagine the cows saying to themselves, "I can't go there. I can see through it. Clearly it will not hold." They are not able to trust. At least, that is my interpretation of the inner life of cows.

I have a more accurate knowledge of the inner lives of people, and I know that it does not take much to evoke fear in us. And I also know that the resurrection is the antidote to anxiety and fear.

Learning to live the resurrection is the issue. Learning to trust that the God of the resurrection will hold us securely is our task. We sometimes have reasons to fear, but we do not need to live in fear. The God who raised our Lord Jesus Christ from the dead will always be active to cast our fear, to roll away the stone of worry, to nudge us into resurrection reality.

Do not be alarmed. Do not be afraid. Christ is risen. He is risen indeed.

Questions to Help You Walk Further Than This Chapter Can Go

1. Can you recall a time recently when you were filled with fear? Can you think of a time when the life of your congregation has been dominated by anxiety?

2. After identifying such a time, use the above four-part analysis of fear to examine what happened. Which of the four factors seemed to have dominated the fear?

3. What would living the resurrection look like for you in that situation? What would need to change in you and in your church to enter into a resurrection reality? What stands in the way of that happening?

4. How might you make "Do not be afraid" a more integral part of your life and the life of your parish? What strategies do you need to develop? How can you be an angelic messenger to others by telling them "Do not be afraid"?

chapter 3

Not Enough to Go Around

The last parish I served in West Virginia had a deservedly earned high reputation for the lunches and dinners they laid out on special occasions. These were usually potluck affairs, but to those who dined they seemed like a meal at a gourmet bistro. At one such function I noticed that a group of the long-time members were huddled together, and an atmosphere of concern seemed to envelope them. I worked my way to them and casually asked one of the group what was happening. "We are practicing family hold-back," she replied. That was a new term to me, so I asked about its meaning. She said, "It's when people don't take any food until we know there is enough to go around."

Many of us practice family hold-back, and we do so not just at the dinner table. We are often plagued by the sense that there is not enough to go around—not enough of what we believe to be important parts of our lives. We are apprehensive that there may not be enough money, time, resources, energy, talent—you name it, and we fear a scarcity of it.

We have just discussed fear. This sense of scarcity is a variation on the theme of fear and anxiety. Our perception that we live in scarcity is a specific form of fear, a fear that challenges us to ponder why we believe we lack what we need.

Please understand that I am not trying to suggest that this sense of scarcity is silly or without foundation. Most of us have passed through times in our lives when the "pickins were slim." For instance, I recall a summer while I was in seminary when I ran out of money, and had to make do with cans of chicken soup and White Castle burgers. I worried about my next meal, and I did so with good cause.

My office is next to a city park. Hidden in the trees in a quiet corner is a place where homeless people tend to gather. My guess is that they assemble there exactly so that other people will not see them. This is a story that repeats itself all over our country: in the secluded corners are many without sufficient food, clothes, shelter, and medical attention. Further, recent economic events have shown that a large part of our population is only one or two paychecks away from sharing in this situation. This touches our hearts, and it scares us. There may not be enough.

As I have said, I spend a significant part of my time with the clerical and lay leaders of the congregations of the diocese. As a result I can assure you that this attitude of scarcity flourishes in our churches, and not just in Montana. The discussion often starts with a question about why that church down the road is growing and our church is not. Typically we then launch into an inventory of what we lack: people, money, time, energy, and especially that mysterious "X factor" that would allow us to attract people. In those moments I am sharply aware that I share with these people a heavy responsibility for the health and vitality of that congregation. I know their worry, and I have to admit that I have no easy or quick solutions to their various kinds of scarcity. We together simply know that there is not enough to go around.

To top it off is the reality of death, the ultimate diminishment. We are painfully aware that all things come to an end. People simply run out of life. And studies in the last decades have shown that congregations, too, have life cycles, and that one of the inevitable stages of that cycle is death. Beneath all of our fears about scarcity is the brutal reality of death and decay. We are frightened and anxiety ridden by a low-level and persistent drone of death that always sounds in the background. There is not enough of life itself to go around.

So here is where we stand. In the lives of many persons, families, and churches, we look at what we have and at what we need, and we come to the fearful conclusion that we may not be able to make ends meet. We may well live our lives in a perpetual state of family hold-back.

The gospel according to John narrates a resurrection story that I have always found both profound and intriguing. That charismatic teacher and miracle worker Jesus had died and been buried. This turn of events stunned the inner circle of Jesus' followers, the apostles; they had in a real way bet their lives on this man. Further, there had been reports and events that suggested Jesus had been raised from the dead. As scholars such as N.T. Wright have shown, the whole category of resurrection was not a factor in their expectation about or understanding of death in general and of Jesus' death in particular. The idea of resurrection did not enter their minds. Little wonder, then, that the apostles seem to be able to walk away from these strange reports. They just knew that their great vision had petered out when the stone had been rolled over the entrance to Jesus' tomb. So, they decide to return home to Galilee. In a comment that is both humorous and poignant, the chief apostle Peter says, "I'm going fishing."

We dare not miss the implications of this. If they were going fishing, that meant that they were returning to their old, pre-Jesus life. He had once called them to leave their nets and boats and follow him as fishers of people, but now they had returned to their former ways. Further, the life of fishermen could be shot through with a sense of scarcity. If they were to survive, they needed to catch fish and lots of them.

But then a resurrection transformation occurs. Here is how the evangelist tells it:

> Just after daybreak, Jesus stood on the beach; but the disciples did not know that it was Jesus. Jesus said to them, "Children, you have no fish, have you?" They answered him, "No." He said to them, "Cast the net to the right side of the boat, and you will find some." So they cast it, and now they were not able to haul it in because there were so many fish. That disciple whom Jesus loved said to Peter, "It is the Lord!" . . . [Peter] hauled the net ashore, full of large fish, a hundred fifty-three of them; and though there were so many, the net was not torn." (John 21:4–7a, 11b)

What can we say about such an amazing turn of events? Here, I believe, is the heart of the matter. When the God who raised Jesus from the dead is at work, there is plenty of what we need to go around. Family hold-back does not apply. The resurrection God provides what resurrection people need to lead resurrection lives.

But we cannot stop yet. Prior to this episode on the seashore, the evangelist narrates another profound story that takes place on Easter evening in Jerusalem.

> When it was evening on that day, the first day of the week, and the doors of the house where the disciples had met were locked

for fear of the Jews, Jesus came and stood among them and said, "Peace be with you." After he said this, he showed them his hands and his side. Then the disciples rejoiced when they saw the Lord. Jesus said to them again, "Peace be with you. As the Father has sent me, so I send you." When he had said this, he breathed on them and said to them, "Receive the Holy Spirit." (John. 20:19–22)

This Easter evening episode clearly demonstrates the Paschal Mystery in action. Note the God-powered movements from fear and death to life and mission. The disciples are emotionally and physically locked in fear. And it is not an irrational fear; what had happened to Jesus on the cross might happen to them if the authorities discovered them. But in a moment of surpassing wonder, the Risen Lord comes into their presence and gives them the gift of peace. And more gifts follow. He breathes on them and says, "Receive the Holy Spirit." Jesus is granting them the supreme gift of his own resurrection presence.

If we can understand the Holy Spirit to be the invisible yet real presence of God, then Jesus is freely bestowing on them his presence in such a mode that his presence is not limited by time and space. This act of breathing on the disciples is reminiscent of the event in Genesis 2, where God molds the shape of a human being out of mud, breathes on it, and thus makes it a living being. In that room in Jerusalem on Easter evening, the new creation was beginning. The reign of God was breaking into the world. In this event, humanity has been allowed to begin the journey back to Eden, where all that was needed was abundantly supplied.

The God of the resurrection provides resurrection people with an abundance of all they need to live resurrection lives and to be agents of God's resurrection mission in the world. We have no need for family hold-back for fear of scarcity. The resurrection of our Lord is the paradigm of the way God works. Resurrection means fullness and abundance of life—all of life.

We now can look at some ramifications of these two resurrection narratives. Implicit in these gospel stories is a three-part invitation. First, we are invited to develop an awareness that we share in the resurrection life of our Lord. This is our state of being by virtue of our baptism into the Paschal Mystery of the dying and rising of Christ. As baptismal people, we become resurrection people and living embodiments of the Paschal Mystery.

Many churches have placed their baptismal fonts in the center of the entry area of the church. You can't enter without walking around the font, that is, you can't enter without being called to an awareness of baptism and resurrection. Some people take it a step further. They dip their fingers into the water in the font and cross themselves as they walk by. In this act they are reminding themselves that they have, in baptism, been marked with the cross of Christ forever and thereby also share in his resurrection. Whether we put our fonts in the entryway and cross ourselves with baptismal water is not as important as the absolute need to keep the font experience in the forefront of awareness as the pattern of the way we are to live. The baptismal life postulates that there will always be enough of all we need to be baptismal people.

Second, we have an invitation in the two gospel stories to test out resurrection living. These narratives say, "Give it a test drive in your life and in the life of your church." When we begin to think scarcity, bring that to awareness, reject it, and move on to resurrection thinking. At that church dinner I mentioned earlier, we had more than enough food. The lady who had explained the concept of family hold-back later said, "I guess we always have had enough food for everyone." Indeed. That summer in seminary when I ran out of money, I managed to get along and certainly did not waste away because of lack of nutrition. These are, of course, small instances. We can think bigger than that. In fact, big thinking and big expectations are an integral part of living in the resurrection.

In the congregation I last served, we had reached an impasse. There were several ministry projects that we needed to carry out, but to do so would mean unbalancing the budget. Never in the history of that church had the vestry voted to let spending exceed the budgeted income. The discussion at that vestry meeting was long and hard, but in the end they bit the bullet and voted to go ahead with the projects. At the end-of-the-year review, we learned from the treasurer that income had exceeded the needs of the budget and that we had some money to spare. I reminded the vestry members of their struggle months earlier. "Congratulations. We have learned that God supplies what we need to be the church," I said.

I have intentionally included this episode about budgets in the church. The budgeting and decision-making processes are key areas in the life of congregations and, therefore, important arenas for testing the reliability of the resurrection. More often than I like to admit, I see vestries and other leadership bodies in the church getting things upside-down. They begin with the resources they believe they have, and then proceed to talk about their mission and ministry. The proper staring point is discerning the mission and ministries that the Risen One wants us to carry out in his name, and then and only then proceed to discuss finding resources. To clerical and lay leaders of the church especially, I offer this challenge: Go ahead. Give it a try. Test the resurrection.

Third, we are invited to learn gratitude. I am convinced that resurrection gratitude is a key component to maturity in the spiritual life. Once we begin to develop an awareness of the resurrection generosity of God, once we begin to trust and test the reality of the Paschal Mystery, the more we will understand that God daily gives us a multitude of reasons to be grateful people. Learning to be grateful is not optional. It is part of the process of becoming mature people of the resurrection. Gratitude is the gasoline that powers our journey with and to the Risen One.

Gratitude, however, does not come easily or naturally. Anyone who has raised children knows the truth of that. When my daughters were small, a familiar versicle between us was:

Dad: What do you say?

Daughters (sighing): Thank you.

We all have to work at gratitude to the God of the resurrection. Becoming thankful people is as important to the maturing of our inner lives as drinking milk is to a developing child. It is a habit of the heart that we need to cultivate.

I have found that using prayer beads has been enormously helpful in my becoming a more grateful person. I begin by going around the circle of beads, using each bead to name someone or something, large or small, for which I am grateful. I am grateful, for instance, for my wife, but also for the comfortable chair in which I sit. Both large matters and small matters are the components of our lives, and are, therefore, worthy of a word of thanks to God. Part of my discipline includes reserving a special bead to prompt an intentional prayer of gratitude for the resurrection of Christ. As a Baby Boomer, gratitude does not come easily, but this little discipline has been an instance of resurrection transformation in my life.

When I was a child, my parents, my sister, and I often went to dinner after church at grandmother's house. And what dinners they were! She didn't use recipes or cookbooks; she just cooked. More than a half-century later, I can still recall the tastes and smells of those meals. It would take hundreds of words, for example, for me to do justice to her pineapple upside-down cake with homemade whipped cream. But here was the odd thing about those gatherings. She and my grandfather never knew who might show up. Every meal had a changing cast of relatives and friends, but this never worried her. "There will be plenty," she would say. And there always was.

I am not suggesting irresponsible living or a magical view of God's actions in our lives. As we noted earlier, we all have and will face situations of genuine scarcity. But if we stop at the point of awareness of what we lack, if we simply shrug the shoulders and give up, we will be cutting ourselves out of the adventure of resurrection living. For instance, when I was in college I wanted to be part of our famous choir. But I did not even attempt to win a spot in the baritone section. I simply told myself, "I don't have a good enough voice." Looking back, I regret that I did not give it a try. I was convinced that I lacked sufficient quality in my singing voice. I suspect that I could have made it, and what an adventure that would have been!

You sense my enthusiasm about and commitment to this implication of Easter. That does not mean, however, that I have forgotten the genuine scarcity of food, shelter, and medical care in many parts of the world. You and I see that, both in the communities in which we live and in the TV news clips from around the world. And I admit that this tragic situation can certainly be interpreted as a challenge to my argument. I do not have a simple answer, but I do remember a newspaper cartoon from years ago. One character says, "Why does God allow so much hunger?" The other character replies, "I'm afraid God would ask me the same question." We might conclude that part of our ministry as the baptized is to be agents of resurrection by addressing both the scarcity we see and the societal structures that allow such a situation to exist. I believe there is plenty to go around, if we are willing to share it.

Furthermore, we do well to distinguish between what we want and what we, in fact, need to be people of the God of the resurrection. When I ask my wife what she wants, she sometimes says, "A brick made out of gold." That is not going to happen. God is not going to provide such a thing. I am suggesting, however, that we give careful attention to the two resurrection stories in John's gospel. There we see a generous God who seems to want to do nothing more than bless us. Resurrection implies an abundance of life and the ability to provide it. We will be given what we need to live as disciples of the Risen Lord. We will be provided with what we need to grow up into Christ. Churches will have what they need to carry out the mission God has called them to. You can count on it—you can build your future on it. As my grandmother used to say, "There will be plenty."

Questions to Help You Explore Resurrection Abundance

1. Can you think of instances of unexpected "gifts" appearing in your life and the life of your church?

2. What are some ways by which you could exercise your muscles so as to develop a stronger trust in God's resurrection generosity?

3. In the John 21 resurrection story, what might be the significance of the 153 fish? What might it symbolize?

4. If you were to decide to become a person who wants to live in the resurrection, what form would your gratitude and generosity take?

chapter 4

MapQuest

Several years back I was in New York City on business. I had a free afternoon, so I decided to visit some bookstores in lower Manhattan. I thought to myself, "I've been here dozens of times, and I can get along without a subway map." So I descended the steps into the subway, bought my pass, and set out on my literary adventure. I managed to get off the train at the right station for one bookstore, but after that I lost my way. I abandoned my efforts with the subway because I was not certain about the location of the bookstores relative to the subway stations. So I set out on foot, thinking I knew the locations of other good stores, but I never did find them. I wandered around for hours, wishing I had been smart enough to get a map. Later that afternoon, I returned to my hotel tired, disgusted with myself, and suffering from calloused feet. What I had hoped would be an adventure had turned into an aimless ordeal. Where is MapQuest when you need it?

That life is a journey, a trek into the future, has become a commonplace image in our culture. In recent years many books have appeared using that image. But some authors have refined the idea by adding the idea that the journey should be understood as being divided into stages. In each stage some important aspect of our life's work needs to occur, we are told, before we can continue the trek into the next stage of our lives. One major stage happens when people are in high school and college. The issue that they need to clarify is what they will do with their lives. What is my aim in life? To what do I want to commit my time and talents? What will be the map for the rest of my days?

I have found this concept of life stages very helpful. But my own variation on this theme, culled from decades of pastoral ministry, is that the question is not asked just by young people, but presents itself again and again in various guises as we walk into the future. A sign of this is revealed in the phenomenon of the majority of people in this country changing jobs two or three times in the course of their working careers.

Moreover, we often say to ourselves, "I hope I am doing the right thing," or "I regret that particular part of my life." From time to time we lose our ability to see a clear vision of our purpose in life. And we sense that it is a blessed person, indeed, who can say at the end of life, "I regret nothing I have done." For most of us, however, the issue of our life's direction persists.

So, the issue of purpose poses itself repeatedly in our journey. Where am I going? What plans and pledges do I need to make to insure the future? Am I wasting my time? Will I be able to deal with the unexpected if it occurs? It's then that we wish we had some sort of existential MapQuest to guide us along our way.

It is not just individuals who ask this question. Churches continually are working on the issue of purpose, direction, and aim, whether they know it or not. I find myself sometimes posing these questions to leaders of churches: What is your purpose as an assembly of Christ's resurrection people? Where do you want to go? What mission do you believe the Risen One is calling you to do? These are tough questions, and answers do not come easily. Most of us have some difficulty envisioning the purpose and direction of our own lives, not to mention that of an organization. And even if we are able to sense where the congregation or diocese ought to steer, we tend to have diverging and even disagreeing perceptions from others about the aims of that given parish.

The distinguished and venerable first Bishop of Montana was the Rt. Rev. Daniel Sylvester Tuttle. He worked long and hard during the last half of the nineteenth century to establish and sustain churches in the geographically vast state of Montana. Years after he had finished his ministry in the Rocky Mountain West, he wrote his memoirs, a fascinating book entitled, *Missionary to the Mountain West*. It is available even now.

Bishop Tuttle's *modus operandi* was to arrive in a town or settlement by horse, stage coach, or train, and settle into that town for a time. He would announce his presence in the local paper, by handbills, and by word-of-mouth. He would preach, baptize, confirm, marry, and bury people. After this initial stage, he would call a meeting and ask those assembled if they sensed a call from God to form a congregation under his jurisdiction. The bishop would add that if they could pledge six hundred dollars a year, he would be able to supply them a priest. In many places, people sensed the call and accepted Bishop Tuttle's challenge.

Part of what has fascinated me about this approach is that Tuttle never had to state a case for having a church, nor did he have to assist people to perceive the mission of the church. Folks by and large accepted the fact that a church was a good thing to have in a community, and they were pretty clear about what that congregation and its priest were to do. Even those who had never darkened the door of a church knew what a church was supposed to do. The ground was fertile, and Bishop Tuttle planted the seed.

We live in a different world. Many in our culture see no need for a church, and care little about its purpose and aim. Establishing new churches is hard work and takes years to accomplish. We have in the last half-century entered a new time, when the general culture no longer seems to understand the need for the church. For instance, there were about a hundred and thirty students in my class in my small hometown's school. With one exception, everyone—everyone—went to church and Sunday School, and that one exception was mocked because he did not attend worship. Being a church member was simply what one did. But clearly our situation has changed. We are a thoroughly secular society, and the church receives little support from our society. Indeed, in some places the church lives and works in a negative climate.

I have noted this story about Bishop Tuttle and contrasted his work with ours today because I firmly believe this distinction has large and direct effects on both our personal and ecclesiastical sense of purpose, mission, and aim. All of the cultural support we have had in the Western world since the fourth century is gone. No one "out there" will supply our reason for existence. No one "out there" has a clear and simple sense of why churches exist or why individuals might want to be part of a church. To use the phrase made popular by William Willimon and Stanley Hauerwas, we Christians are resident aliens.[1]

We do not fit into our culture. Even individuals trying to live with integrity—Christian or not—find little help with the issue

---

1. Stanley Hauerwas and William Willimon, *Resident Aliens: A Provocative Assessment of Culture and Ministry for People Who Know that Something is Wrong* (Nashville, TN: Abingdon Press, 1989).

of purpose and direction apart from our culture's shrill advocacy of shallow materialism.

We are lost without a map. We are on a journey, but the aim of it is by no means clear.

The church of the first century, that is, the church of the New Testament, lived in a similar climate. There were not cultural rewards for being a Christian; in fact, at times Christians faced punishment for their faith. And individuals, too, lived in a world of many languages, many cultures, and many appeals for their commitment. The question of purpose was not answered from without, by the society or culture, but had to be dealt with from within one's own self.

Several stories from the New Testament lay out the path these Christians took on their journey. It was a journey we need to see in steps or stages. These stories can be invaluable to us as we try to answer the lifelong question of purpose. Let's begin with the initial step of that New Testament journey to purpose.

We begin with a small section of St. Paul's letter to the church in the busy port city of Corinth. They, like us, had trouble getting their minds around the idea of resurrection and its implication. To help them understand, Paul quotes what appears to be an early creedal statement about Easter. The language he uses suggests that he had learned this word by word in the same way that people today memorize the Lord's Prayer or the Nicene Creed. Here is what he says:

> For I handed on to you as of first importance what I in turn had received: that Christ died for our sins in accordance with the scriptures, and that he was buried, and that he was raised on the third day in accordance with the scriptures, and that he appeared to Cephas, then to the twelve. Then he appeared to more than

five hundred brothers and sisters at one time, most of whom are still alive . . . Then he appeared to James, then to all the apostles. Last of all, as to one untimely born, he appeared also to me. (1 Cor. 15:3–8)

This is an extraordinarily rich passage, and one could write whole books about it. But for us, it is enough to note this overriding point: the Risen Christ seeks out people. He makes his way to where they are, and appears to them. Paul lists the names of some of these people, noting that most are still alive at the time he was writing. Therein lies an implicit invitation to talk with these people and question them about these resurrection events. They will tell you, Paul says, that the Risen One came to them and appeared to them. This is the first stage in our journey through the New Testament story.

In the gospel of Luke, we find signs of the second step. The Risen Lord has appeared and spoken to a number of the disciples in various places. The final word is this: "And see, I am sending upon you what my Father promised; so stay here in the city until you have been clothed with power from on high" (Luke 24:49). The city is, of course, Jerusalem, and the promised gift is the Holy Spirit, the invisible yet real presence of the Resurrected One.

A further instance of the second step happens in the gospel according to John. The apostles and other disciples have gathered in a room in Jerusalem, and have locked the doors for fear that they, like Jesus, would be arrested and executed. Then, the Risen Lord appears and "breathed on them and said to them, 'Receive the Holy Spirit. If you forgive the sins of any, they are forgiven them; if you retain the sins of any, they are retained'" (John 20:22–23).

The elements of this story are similar to the one in Luke. The Spirit is given and they receive instructions about the future. In this Lucan account the instructions deal with the forgiveness and the retaining or losing of sins. The effect of these words is that now the apostles and others should take up the ministry of Jesus, the ministry of reconciliation and of judgment as their purpose and direction.

Now we have made a second step on our journey to purpose. First, the Risen Lord seeks out his disciples, in particular the apostles who will eventually become the founders of the church. Second, Jesus gives the Holy Spirit. Again, this stands as a very rich promise that would yield much fruit from further study. But for our purposes it suffices to say that we can count on the real presence of the Risen One, even if we cannot see, sense, or feel that presence.

The climax of the gospel of Matthew lays before us the third step. The Risen Christ meets his apostles on a mountain in Galilee. He gives them authority to carry on his work, and tells them to make disciples by teaching and baptism. Then the evangelist records his final words: "And remember, I am with you always, to the end of the age" (Matthew 28:20).

I understand this promise as an absolutely essential part of the journey. Not only does Christ seek out his people and gift them with the Holy Spirit, but further promises that he, the Risen One, will be with them always. The presence of Christ is not to be seen as a fleeting thing, a here-today-gone-tomorrow phenomenon. The promise extends into the future, all of the future. It stands so clear and firm that one can trust it, can step into an unknown future with confidence, can build one's life on it.

The last step in our small journey has been both implicit and explicit in all the above stories. At all points, the Risen One gives his followers work to do. In a sidebar to these events, the writer of the gospel of Luke adds this detail in the book of the Acts of the Apostles, the sequel to his gospel:

> When [Jesus] had said this, as they were watching, he was lifted up, and a cloud took him out of their sight. While he was going and they were gazing up toward heaven, suddenly two men in white robes stood by them. They said, "Men of Galilee, why do you stand looking up toward heaven?" (Acts 1:9–11)

I admit that I find this humorous. Don't just stand there, say the angelic messengers. Do something. It reminds me of the bumper sticker: *Jesus is coming again. Look busy.* And we, in fact, are given much to do, a clear purpose, goal, and aim.

As noted above in Matthew's gospel, the apostles are told to do four things:

- Go to all peoples and nations.
- Make disciples of all peoples and nations.
- Baptize them.
- Teach them to obey Jesus and his teaching.

This is a big assignment, but it is certainly clear enough.

In Mark's gospel, the three terrified women find an angel at the tomb of Jesus, and that being tells them to give their testimony to Jesus' disciples. They would be able to report:

- that they had encountered an angel,
- that the tomb was empty,
- that the angel proclaimed the resurrection of Jesus from the dead, and

- that the disciples are to go to Galilee where the Risen Christ will meet them.

We are told that in their terror they tell nothing to anyone. Nevertheless, they are given the work of witnessing to their experience of resurrection. Speaking the good news is their job.

In the gospel of Luke, the disciples are told to wait for the gift of the power of the Holy Spirit. They stay in Jerusalem, and soon enough they experience this gift of divine power and presence. These events, which are recorded in the book of Acts, note that the first thing they do is to begin to proclaim the Paschal Mystery to all within their hearing. As with Matthew and Mark, the elements of proclaiming and teaching are central, and the focus of these activities is anyone and everyone. The ministry of Jesus is announced so that in a genuine sense the story goes on, the work of Jesus happens over and over again in and through their words. Their ministry enables others to live the resurrection.

And in John's gospel, Jesus appears, grants the proto-church gathered in the locked room the gifts of peace, of the presence of the Spirit, and a charge to carry on his work of reconciliation and forgiveness.

We are MapQuest people, often not sure where we are going or why. Part of the good news of Easter and of living the resurrection is that the Risen Lord has given us a noble purpose and direction. The resurrection supplies God's response to our persistent question about purpose and meaning. From the resurrection we discover two implications for our personal journeys and for the life of the church.

First, we must be clear about whom we belong to. We must be certain of our identity. Those who travel by air know that establishing identity is an absolutely necessary step in making a journey today. We have to produce a driver's license, passport, or an official ID for the security guards. And the name on the card must match the name on the boarding pass, and the picture on the ID must match your own face. Only then comes the word, "OK. You can go."

For Christian people, identity is rooted in baptism. It is no accident that one of the fascinating aspects of the baptismal liturgy is its careful attention to names. The priest asks what the person is to be named, and at the moment of baptism a name is bestowed along with the application of the water. This is why our given or first names used to be commonly called our Christian names. The naming aspect of this sacrament helps us understand that we now belong to Christ, that we have been purchased at a price, that we are united to Christ in his death and resurrection, that we are known individually and by name, and all this, therefore, establishes our basic identity.

As an activity at retreats, I sometimes pass out paper and pens, and ask people to make a list of words that they use to identify themselves. In my case, the list would include: husband, father, sibling, male, American, educated, and so on. Baptism says to us that the first identifier on that list should be baptized or Christian or disciple of Christ. Our baptismal identity precedes and trumps all other factors.

To be a person with a sense of purpose in life, with a perception that life has a meaning and mission, we first must know who we are at the foundation of our lives. The same is true for churches. Parishes—and denominations—must be able to say to themselves and to the world, "We are a community in which you can encounter and be encountered by the Risen Lord. Christ is alive in and among us." Churches also need to proclaim, "Our mission and ministry reproduces the mission and ministry of the Crucified and Risen One. His work is our work. And you can be involved in that with us."

I need to add that no one congregation can exemplify all the aspects of Christ's ministry. No one parish has all of the talents, skills, resources to do that. But each one has some talents and skills and can carry out some parts of Jesus' work.

Individuals, parishes, and denominations should be very clear about these two factors of identity and purpose. We should be able to state these things to ourselves and others in simple and short ways. One of the popular phrases from the '60s was "consciousness-raising"; this usually was a call to be clear and conversant about the issues of race and war. We need to raise awareness to our level of our identity, our purpose, our goal. We need to know down to the roots of our being that we are on a journey with and to the Risen Lord.

If you watch TV even a little, you may have been struck by the effective and powerful recruiting ads produced by the U.S. Navy. They begin with scenes that seem to be from a vivid video game, except that in the ad we do not see gaming mayhem but rather sailors involved in a risky rescue mission. Then comes the slogan: "America's Navy—A Global Force for Good." I imagine that this must be enormously powerful for young people dealing with the question of purpose. Here the Navy holds up images of being involved in something bigger than one's self, in something that requires one's best efforts and deepest commitment, and in something that can make the world better.

With due respect, the Navy can't hold a candle to the life of discipleship. We all are invited to baptism, and to living out our baptism identity with our best efforts and deepest commitment. We all are asked to be aware that no one less than the Risen Lord makes this invitation. We all are called to not simply make the world better, but to be agents of resurrection for the transformation of the whole world.

We have no need to be MapQuest people. We know who we are. We know what we are to do.

Questions by Which to Explore the Purpose of Our Life Journey

1. Can you find in yourself times and occasions when you seem to be spinning your wheels, where life is less than meaningful and abundant? Describe the times and explore what they might indicate about your life.

2. How do you react to the concept of our purpose as persons and as a church being work, the work of reproducing Jesus' ministry?

3. What skills, talents, experiences, training, interests, and education could you offer to the Risen Lord as an agent of resurrection? What are the gifts, interests, and skills in your church that could make it a resurrection community of transformation?

4. In practical terms, describe what it means to give one's best to a cause.

chapter 5

You Can't Change the Past

Most people who find themselves traveling by air these days have learned to grin and bear the difficulties and indignities of plane flight. Little wonder that at nearly every informal event I attend, several people seem to be compelled to share horror stories of recent flights. Because I do have to fly often, I have learned to try to make the best of it. For me this means securing an aisle seat with leg-stretching room and having lots of reading material at hand. This allows me to withdraw into the book without risk of interruption. On occasion, however, the person next to me breaks into my reverie with the words, "Please excuse me," as they rise to make their way to the aisle. Most of the time I simply reply, "No problem," and stand up.

"No problem" can be a proper response to the small irritants in life. But we experience many occasions where we simply cannot use that phrase. Some of the words and actions of others make us want to shout, "I have a big problem with that." The fact of the matter is that we often encounter attitudes, actions, and comments that cut us to the quick, that injure and bruise us at the center of our beings, that evoke some of our strongest feelings of anger and pain. Sometimes others go too far, violate too many boundaries, inflict too much hurt, indulge in too much outrageous behavior. Sadly, we need to add that the church is not immune to this sort of behavior.

One afternoon, one of the less-active members of the church I was serving simply appeared at the door to my office. He was beside himself, sobbing from emotional injury. Earlier that afternoon his wife of many years announced that she had found a job and that she was divorcing him. Between the tears he said, "I thought we had a good marriage. I never saw this coming." A brief conversation had shaken his life to its foundations, and I suspect that he has spent the rest of his life trying to live with the pain of rejection and promises broken. The words and actions of that day have shaped in deep ways how he will face every new day. We all experience the pain of big problems and big injuries, and we can't get away from the results of those times, because they have become a part of who we are.

We can all quickly and easily recall events of pain, fear, and anger in our lives; the memories spring to mind with no effort. Indeed, our problem is trying to remember to forget those episodes. Furthermore, we feel more shame and pain when we recall the times when we have been the source of the pain and anger in others. We have all inflicted pain and anguish on others, and ironically it is often on those about whom we care the most. So, we live with the shame and guilt involved with those memories, in addition to the hurt caused us by others. We can lay it down as a firm fact of life, an inevitable part of being a human being, something we can do nothing about.

Those of us who are involved in the life of the church know that it, too, can be a forum for both giving and receiving hurtful words, attitudes, and actions. People sometimes tell me,

"There is no fight like a church fight," and I readily agree. I suspect that part of the reason we say that is because we expect more from the people who associate themselves with congregations. We sing, "They will know we are Christians by our love," but we find too little evidence of that virtue. We like to say that our churches are friendly and accepting communities, but then we too often proceed to prove the opposite. And we can point to too many instances where this happens so much that parishes become toxic, congregations that are bad for your inner health.

And it can get worse. People, both lay and ordained, can become so involved in the giving and receiving of hurt that they plow a church into the ground to such a degree that it takes a whole generation to recover. Building a vital, resurrection congregation takes years of prayer, commitment, and hard work, but a conflict of only a month or two's duration can literally kill a church. And even if the congregation manages to survive, it will take several decades to recover its health. These hard times usually take root because of one of two factors. The fight is caused by someone or a small group that tries to exercise undue power, or by someone or a group trying to protect their turf. And then we use words and actions like weapons of war to attack the opponents, who also happen to be brothers and sisters in Christ. I hasten to add that all of this can apply to whole dioceses. Under these circumstances, guilt and shame, fear and defensiveness abound and become a permanent part of the record of that church.

I had taken my dog to the veterinarian for an exam and shots. In the waiting room I quickly noticed that a very nervous lady was holding her dog on her lap. I thought to myself, "That is the strangest-looking breed I have ever seen." It had a huge, bulbous nose. The vet appeared to talk with the woman, and her story quickly came out. That morning she had been jogging with her dog, they had encountered a rattlesnake, and the snake had bitten the dog on its nose. Now I understood why she was so anxious and why the dog had that huge snout. The woman was desperate for an antidote for the bite. "Can't you give her a shot?" she pleaded. The veterinarian calmly explained that snake bite antidotes cost over a thousand dollars per injection, and, furthermore, the hospital would not sell the medicine for use on an animal. But then came the good news. The doctor said, "Dogs have an innate immunity to snake bites, even poisonous ones. Just take the dog home. It doesn't need an antidote. She will be fine."

The antidote to those painful words and actions that we both give and receive is forgiveness. Unlike a dog with a snake bite, we have no immunity to hurt and guilt; indeed, we have an innate sensitivity to such things, so that they become a permanent part of who we are. Only forgiveness will offer a cure, and it can be both expensive and rare.

Once again, a resurrection story can guide us to understand both the nature of forgiveness and how it works in our lives. The twenty-first chapter of John's gospel contains two beautiful and profound stories about resurrection and forgiveness. The story begins in the time following Easter morning. And again the apostles have made the journey north to Galilee. In this episode we find them on the shore of the Sea of Tiberius, as John calls it; it is more commonly called the Sea of Galilee. Peter declares to the group that he is going fishing; this act represents a return to his former way of life, his familiar pre-Jesus life. We may go so far as to say that this may suggest that he is giving up his loyalty to the work of Jesus. The disciples spend the night on the water, but are not able to catch anything. As the sun rises, a figure on the shore says, "Children, you have no fish, have you?" They reply in the negative, and he instructs them to fish off the right side of the boat. Although it is an odd suggestion, they do it, and the result is that they catch so many fish, they are not able to haul the full nets into their boat. It is at this point that the disciple whom Jesus loved (the tradition of the church calls him John, but, in fact, in the gospel his proper name is never mentioned; rather he is simply called "the disciple whom Jesus loved") has a flash of insight. "It is the Lord!" he shouts, and the group begins to make its way to the shore.

Now the first of the two forgiveness episodes begin.

> When they had gone ashore, they saw a charcoal fire there, with fish on it, and bread . . . Jesus said to them, "Come, and have breakfast." Now none of the disciples dared to ask him, "Who are you?" because they knew it was the Lord. Jesus came and took the bread and gave it to them, and did the same with the fish. This was now the third time that Jesus appeared to the disciples after he was raised from the dead. (John 21:9, 12–14)

We see again that the Risen Lord has sought out his followers. He, too, has made his way to Galilee in order to be with them. It is crucial that we remember that these were members of the intimate, inner circle of Jesus' followers, and they had witnessed his work in a first-hand and personal way. With the exception of the beloved disciple, these are also the ones who deserted Jesus during his trial and execution. We can imagine with a good deal of certainty that the disciples were carrying the burden of deep guilt and shame about their failure to stand with their leader, a burden they would never be able to shake. We might conclude that their guilt must have become even more acute as they were in the presence of the now-risen Jesus.

In an act of deep hospitality and acceptance, Jesus prepares and serves them breakfast. Most of us are rather careful about whom we invite to eat with us; we know a meal is an intimate and personal affair that we would not want to share with just anyone. The Latin root for the word "companion," for example, suggests that a companion is exactly someone with whom we share bread. We should not, therefore, underestimate the import of Jesus' forgiveness, demonstrated in the breakfast he has prepared with his own hands.

Furthermore, it would be hard for Christians not to recognize the overtones of the Eucharist in this story. I have no doubt that that implication is just what we are supposed to infer from the story. We understand that nearly every Eucharist leads the congregation into a meal that mediates the presence of the Risen Lord, a time during which we are invited to eat and drink in his presence, and thereby experience divine acceptance and forgiveness. Every Eucharist becomes that resurrection breakfast on the shore of the sea. The gathered disciples that day knew that Jesus had reinstated them as part of his family.

Next, Jesus turns his attention to Peter, who presents an especially difficult case. During Jesus' trial, Peter had attempted to watch the proceedings from outside the door of the high priest's house. Three times those standing with him had identified him as a follower of Jesus, and three times he denied that relationship in emphatic terms. We can wonder what different course of events might have followed if Peter had courageously affirmed his relationship with Jesus; he likely would have died with his master. But now, on the shore we see the leader of the apostles standing before Jesus in a place of deep shame. Then follows a dialog between Jesus and Peter that both must have found painful.

> When they had finished breakfast, Jesus said to Simon Peter, "Simon son of John, do you love me more than these?" He said to him, "Yes, Lord; you know that I love you." Jesus said to him, "Feed my lambs." A second time he said to him, "Simon son of John, do you love me?" He said to him, "Yes, Lord; you know that I love you." Jesus said to him, "Tend my sheep." He said to him the third time, "Simon son of John, do you love me?" Peter felt hurt because he had said to the third time, "Do you love me?" And he said to him, "Lord, you know everything; you know that I love you." Jesus said to him "Feed my sheep." (John 21:15–17)

Some call this story the Rehabilitation of Peter. Surely it is at least that. For every time Peter denied Jesus, he is allowed to reaffirm his love for Jesus. And each time, Jesus assigns Peter a role in the continuing work of the resurrection. Despite the heinous nature of his denial, Jesus reinstates Peter into the fellowship of the resurrection and gives him important work to do. Scripture itself does not tell us exactly what happened to Peter in the subsequent years, but just after the above episode, Jesus delivers a prophecy about the apostle's future. The prediction alone is obscure, but the tradition of the church makes it clear. Long-standing tradition says that Peter did go throughout the Mediterranean world, and in Rome, the center of things at that time, he was crucified and buried. In the end, Peter did share in the judgment and condemnation of Jesus, albeit in a delayed manner.

We have said that the antidote to our guilt, shame, and failure is forgiveness. And in two episodes of John's resurrection narrative we have explored two profound stories about forgiveness. Jesus shows us what forgiveness is and how it works.

The word forgiveness itself suggests a generous gift, a giving of one's self for another. So, in those Johannine stories we see Jesus setting aside his claim to justice, to punishment, to revenge. He does not demand his rights, but rather gives himself, his presence, to his disciples. In both episodes Jesus is acting in such a way that he is present to his failed followers, so that he can offer them himself, and thereby they are enabled to experience acceptance and a renewed, transformed relationship.

It works in the same manner with us. As I have already suggested, we continually find ourselves on the shore, where Jesus has come to seek us out, to accept us, to bless us, and to transform us. This happens most profoundly in the Holy Meal of the Eucharist. The Risen Lord knows us with all of our failures, mistakes, and intentional acts of injury. And yet he makes himself present, feeds us on divine love, and gives us numberless opportunities to be rehabilitated.

So we can declare: forgiveness does, in fact, change the past. Forgiveness uncouples us from the shame and guilt we drag around with us. Forgiveness corrects our distorted vision, so that we can look at the past in a transformed way. Forgiveness proclaims to us that we do not need to be shaped in the present and future by our past.

John Bunyan portrays this change in his magnificent allegory of the Christian life, *Pilgrim's Progress*. We are introduced to the main character, Christian, as he wanders around carrying a heavy burden on his back. Through the words of scripture, he finds his way to a wicket gate, the gate of forgiveness. As he passes through the gate, the burden simply drops off his back. With rejoicing at his new circumstances, Christian sets off on his journey to the Heavenly City. Forgiveness changes the past. Forgiveness sets us free from its burdens and allows us to pursue an open future.

All of this is good news, indeed. If we can internalize forgiveness, we are comforted and transformed into a resurrection way of life. But forgiveness does not end there. In the Lord's Prayer, Jesus lays before us the challenging side of forgiveness. "Forgive us our sins as we forgive those who sin against us." Note well the important linkage between receiving divine forgiveness and being an instrument of forgiveness to those around us. In fact, Jesus says that linkage is so solid that divine forgiveness cannot be active in our lives unless we are willing to become agents of Christ-like forgiveness. We can't receive it unless we can give it. We can't give it until we have received it. It is at this point we can recall that familiar slogan: Christ loves us so much that he accepts us just as we are. But few people seem to know the inevitable second part: Christ loves us so much that he will not let us stay the way we are. We must become agents of forgiveness.

Given that, we can garner four facts about forgiveness from the resurrection stories in John 21. First, even if we are the person offended against, we must take the initiative in establishing forgiveness. As we have noted, Jesus sought out his guilty band of followers. He took the initiative. There is no room here for "I'll forgive her if she apologizes" or "I'll forgive but I will not forget."

This applies to the church as well. In chapter 18 of Matthew's gospel, we find Jesus' plan for conflict management and reconciliation. He says, "If another member of the church sins against you, go and point out the fault when the two of you are alone" (Matt. 18:15). Here again the offended party should not wait for the offenders to come to their senses and apologize. And again, the word is "go"—we are to seek out the other and, between the two, work it out in private. There is not room here for gossip, triangulating, or backstabbing, three common ways we deal with ruptured relations in the church. In following Jesus' plan, we are acting positively as agents of resurrection life, and are both freeing ourselves and others from the past, liberating all for a new future.

Second, we are to forgive. We cannot merely make ourselves be present and go through the motions of a half-hearted attempt to set things right. We are to forgive, to set things right. The fact is that sometimes we do not want to forgive. When we are honest we have to admit that we enjoy playing with our anger. We like to feel aggrieved and misunderstood. We desire others to say to us, "You know, you are entirely in the right, and you are justified in your anger." We should, as the letter to the Ephesians puts it, grow up. Our goal is to become mature Christian people, who can deal with disappointment and hurt in a resurrection, forgiving way. We need to hear it often: our goal is to "grow up" (Eph. 4:15) The ability to forgive is a certain sign that we are maturing in our relationship with the Risen Lord, who is the source of all pardon and mercy.

Third, we need to own up to the fact that forgiveness always costs. In a situation where genuine forgiveness is needed, we will not find ourselves saying, "No problem." The need for forgiveness points to places of deep rupture and concomitant pain, guilt, anger, and shame. Real pardon is never easy. It will require that someone pays an emotional cost to effect a new relationship. We have already said that for Jesus to forgive his disciples, he had to do again what he did most dramatically on the cross. His word was "Forgive them, Father." He stepped outside the cycle of retaliation and strict justice. The emotional cost must have been enormous.

Take the example of a simple argument between two people. We can surmise that power or turf protection are key factors beneath the anger and guilt. The arguers use blame, accusations of unfairness, bullying, leaving the room, and maybe even physical violence. For forgiveness to take effect, someone has to give up his sense of being in the right, of not having to admit responsibility. It's a common situation; we either see arguments or are involved in them almost daily. Because of that we know how hard it is to put self aside, be present, and open the way to a new relationship. Indeed, all of us can think of people who seem unable to pay the price; they cannot forgive. Or, more accurately, they *will not* forgive. Forgiveness always costs. Because we stand in a forgiven relationship with God in Christ, we are in a place of mercy and graciousness that allows us to pick up the tab.

In seminary I had an instructor who taught me an important lesson about what he termed "sacrificial leadership." By this he meant that leaders need to function out of forgiveness, out of the willingness to pay the price, ready to accept blame. This reminds us that forgiveness is never merely personal, but also must be one of the prime directives in the life of churches. This means Christian leaders, ordained and lay, need to be ready to pay the price.

I used to do some teaching in a seminary. One day a student came in with a story about the church luncheon that had taken place the previous Sunday. Some of the people of the church had apparently put some of their pot-luck dishes on a table in the kitchen. It was a hot day, some of the food spoiled, and nearly everyone present became ill that night. The student went on to say that the congregation was now involved in a church-destroying argument—all based on bad potato salad. What might have happened if someone had stepped up and said, "I am sorry. I should have reminded everyone to put their food in the refrigerator"? Or, "I am not sure about it, but my dish may have been the culprit. I am horrified by that, and I apologize." I did not offer any advice to the student, and I do not know how the crisis ended. But this is a case where someone needed to sacrifice, to accept the blame, to pay the cost. This is the only way churches can be restored to health and vigor. This is the way of forgiveness.

Sacrifice is the hard side of forgiveness. But the truth is that all of us have made our way in life this far because of forgiveness and sacrifice. Parents sacrifice sleep to care for a sick child in the middle of the night. Teachers put up with low pay and the hassles of the classroom—they sacrifice—so that students can learn. Marriages endure because both spouses exercise sacrifice and pardon. We may not like it, but we must do it. The Risen One commands it.

Years before I was made a bishop, a fellow priest in the diocese and I had a public disagreement about some matters regarding our bishop. These matters were important for the life of the diocese, and both the other priest and I had thought and prayed long and hard about our positions, with the result that we did not have a simple gentlemen's difference of opinion, but rather we engaged in a genuine and heartfelt clash. I left the argument with the idea that my colleague had not exercised his mind with the logic and clarity that I had. Several days later he called and asked for an appointment. We set a date, and he made the three-hour drive to my study. It was not a pleasant meeting. He sat on the edge of his seat with fists clinched, and I had to consciously remind myself not to shoot off my mouth. At some point in the discussion, he said, "I came here to see you, because Jesus clearly said that we have to forgive and be reconciled. And I am serious about obeying Jesus." This nearly left me speechless. He was in the right and I was not. While we continued to disagree about the actions of the bishop, he had sacrificed an afternoon of his time, had made himself present, and had reminded both me and himself that the Risen Lord is serious—really serious—about reconciliation, pardon, and forgiveness. That act changed the past, and it changed the future.

Forgiveness always comes at an enormous cost, and, when given, opens the door to a life-giving future. It is the Paschal Mystery at work. It is living in the resurrection.

Questions to Help You Live into Resurrection Forgiveness

1. It is hard to be involved in the life of a congregation without having your toes stepped on. Can you recall some occasions when this has happened to you? Recall the feelings and thoughts. What did you do? And be honest with yourself.

2. What would help you be able to develop the ability to forgive?

3. What skills do you have that you can exercise as an agent of forgiveness?

4. Where is the Risen One calling you to forgive and accept forgiveness now?

chapter 6

I Believe in Doubt

O ver the years I have spent many hours standing beside the beds of hospitalized people. There is something about that setting, and about feeling weak and ill, that permits people to speak what is in their hearts in a straightforward way. One of the common comments I heard in that setting was, "I have doubts about God. I wish I had more faith." This is usually accompanied by embarrassment or shame. I suspect that these folks assume that more and better faith would help them through the hard time in which they find themselves. And perhaps a few assume that their illness is a sort of divine response to their feeble faith, a punishment, if you will. Christians, we assume, should be firm in their faith and have a trust in God that is rock solid.

Doubts and questions, then, have a bad name in religious circles. Yet we need to be honest and admit that we all have soft spots in our trust and cracks in our faith. For these reasons, we need to explore the accounts of the resurrection for some guidance. I propose that we take three initial steps with the help of the New Testament, and then try to come to some conclusions about doubt and faith. The three steps are these: an exploration of resurrection stories, a brief discussion about belief in the resurrection of our Lord, and some comments about miracles in general. So, let's take the first step.

At the climax of the gospel according to Matthew, we find the eleven apostles on a mountain in Galilee. They have gathered there at the instruction of the Risen Lord himself. When they are assembled as ordered, Christ is there with them. Note carefully the evangelist's description of what happened next: "When they saw him, they worshipped him; but some doubted" (Matt. 28:17).

I must admit that every time I read that verse, I am shocked at the honesty of it. Here are Jesus' closest followers, the people who knew him best, and they are granted the enormous honor of an encounter with him as the Risen Lord. I find myself saying, "I wish I were there." But then the text states the simple fact that some doubted.

The Greek word translated as doubt has some subtle overtones to it. While "doubt" is the best and simplest translation, the word also suggests a wavering and a sense of uncertainty. The most helpful nuance, I think, is that it can be translated as "second thoughts." At this moment of majestic revelation, even some of the apostles are wavering. I can imagine what their thoughts might be: "Can I trust what I am seeing? It looks like Jesus, but how can that be? I cannot make sense of what is happening here. This is so stunning that I cannot take it in." That is doubt in action.

The major factor we need to note here is that doubt is a category introduced by the New Testament itself into the resurrection accounts. It would appear that faith and doubt go hand in hand. To have faith implies an element of doubt, and doubt implies an element of faith. Even for the apostles this was true.

The twenty-fourth chapter of the gospel of Luke is for me one of the high points in the entire Bible, and it, too, shows us faith and doubt as inseparable partners. The chapter contains a number of resurrection episodes, and we will take up several of these in the order in which they appear.

In the opening episode of the chapter, three of the women who had been devoted followers of Jesus are at the tomb on Sunday morning. They find the tomb empty, and two angels interpret what has happened. The women were "perplexed." The three then scurry off to report to the apostles. Here is how the apostles reacted to the witness of the women: "But these words seemed to them an idle tale, and they did not believe them" (Luke 24:11). The New Jerusalem Bible has a more vivid translation; the report of the women seemed to the apostles to be "pure nonsense." Who could not be shocked at the degree of open honesty in this account? And again, the apostles are, surprisingly, the ones who appear to doubt most strongly.

The chapter continues with the story of the road to Emmaus, in which two disciples meet the Risen Lord on the road, but do not recognize him. They are intrigued by this seeming stranger, and they invite him to share supper with them. At that meal when the bread is broken (a Lucan phrase suggesting eucharistic overtones), they are suddenly able to recognize the Risen Christ at table with them. They hurry back to Jerusalem again to report to the apostles, who themselves tell of an encounter between the Risen Lord and Peter that has taken place in the interim.

While they are discussing all of this, Jesus once again seems simply to be there among them. He salutes them with "Peace be with you," but again they are startled and terrified. At this point Jesus names what is going on with his followers: "Why are you frightened, and why do doubts arise in your hearts?" (Luke 24:38). The apostles apparently believe that they are having a paranormal experience with a ghost (which, I think we have to admit, is an explanation of this unparalleled event that would likely come to our minds, too). He invites them to touch him to confirm that he is a corporeal being, not a ghost. He shows them his hands and side, to convince them that this is the same Jesus they knew and who had died on the cross; this rules out explaining what is happening by saying this is merely someone with an uncanny resemblance to Jesus. But the doubt persists: "they were disbelieving and still wondering" (Luke 24:41). Then he eats some fish, something no ghost can do.

The word for doubt in these passages suggests a going back and forth in one's mind. The Greek term is related to the word for dialog, that sense of saying, "On one hand . . . but on the other hand. Maybe this or maybe that." Who of us has not experienced that sort of doubt?

Surely the big "doubt" story in the New Testament is a resurrection account involving one of the apostles who has forever been known as "doubting Thomas." The events are recorded in chapter 20 of John's gospel. On Easter evening, the Risen Christ has appeared to the apostles and others, but Thomas had not been present. When he heard their witness, Thomas responded adamantly, "Unless I see the mark of the nails in his hands, and put my finger in the mark of the nails and my hand in his side, I will not believe" (John 20:25). In the original Greek that phrase "I will not believe" is stated in the most emphatic form possible. This is doubt multiplied by two.

The following Sunday, Christ appears to Thomas and invites him to touch his wounds, and then adds "Do not doubt but believe" (John 20:27). Thomas then declares his belief in bold terms, "My Lord and my God" (John 20:28). The conclusion of this episode holds great importance, because the Risen One seems to be addressing anyone who is reading or hearing this story. He says, "Blessed are those who have not seen and yet have come to believe" (John 20:29). I can see no other way to explain that comment, apart from noting that the Risen Christ himself acknowledges that doubt is always a companion of belief.

We can conclude the first step in our walk by confessing that doubt and uncertainty, wavering and questioning are openly a part of the New Testament stories about the resurrection. Even those who had a close relationship with Jesus for an extended period of time (one to three years, depending on which gospel you read) and who have been witnesses to the resurrection, in some cases multiple times, still have moments of doubt and uncertainty. As we work on the implications of the resurrection, we should be conscious that the scriptural accounts audaciously state that doubt and uncertainty are part of the experience of living in the resurrection. Given that, perhaps we should not be so hard on ourselves when we find ourselves uncertain.

The second step is to analyze the category of resurrection in a general way. At the outset, I acknowledge that the resurrection cannot be proved. We usually put the question this way, "Did the resurrection really happen? Did something actually and factually occur on that first Easter morning?"

Because we have to say that the resurrection cannot be proved in an absolute sense, doubt quickly sneaks through the door. This state of uncertainty has been enhanced by some scholars who advocated an internalized and psychological explanation of Easter. Their point of view said that the term "resurrection" denotes the understanding of early Christians that Christ's death had opened new ways of understanding God's dealings with humanity. The Lord was resurrected in their minds and hearts, not in any outward or physical way. Although this interpretation appears to me to be on the wane, it nevertheless has exerted a destabilizing influence, and continues to do so. If we are to stand beside Paul in declaring the resurrection to be the central event of the human story, then we need to deal seriously with these ideas.

In reply to these challenges, there are six very suggestive and important items we need to consider:

- No one was an eyewitness to the resurrection itself. No one was in the tomb with Jesus to report on what happened during the night. Christian art is provocative about this. In the icon tradition of the Orthodox Church, there are two images considered appropriate for display at Easter: first, the visit of the women to the tomb, and second, the harrowing of hell, which pictures Jesus kicking down the gates of hell and reaching out to rescue Adam and Eve from their coffins. Note there is no portrayal of the events inside the tomb itself. In Western sacred art, I am aware of only a couple of paintings of the actual resurrection, one by Matthias Grünewald and another by Fra Angelico. No one witnessed the events in the tomb, and, in fact, if we are to judge by the paucity of paintings, even those most imaginative of people, artists, have difficulty comprehending it.

- What we do have are two items. The first involves the many accounts of the discovery of the empty tomb. In and of themselves, the accounts are provocative, and are necessary but not conclusive to whether the resurrection happened. But more important than the empty tomb are the resurrection appearances during a relatively short period of time after Easter. Part of the value of that early creedal statement in 1 Corinthians, which we considered earlier, is that Paul has a checklist of the appearance of the Risen Lord to various people. He significantly notes to the people in Corinth at the time he is writing (probably around AD 55) that most of these people are still alive. As noted before, he is by implication saying, therefore, you can go and talk to them and hear their witnesses. Both the facts of the empty tomb and the appearances allow us to affirm the possibility of the bodily resurrection of Jesus.

- The gospel writers are clearly aware that the resurrection poses serious problems, and they try to deal with these issues. I believe it is fair to say that if we were among those early followers of Jesus and heard about the empty tomb and the appearances, resurrection would not be the first thing to come to mind. It would be easier to say that someone had stolen the body of Jesus or that he had not really died on the cross but revived in the cool darkness of the tomb. So, the gospels note that the Roman soldiers present at the cross reported officially to the Roman governor that Jesus had died; the soldiers had no reason to state anything other than their perception of the facts, and they were, after all, experts on death. Furthermore, Matthew's gospel says that not only was the entrance to the tomb blocked by a heavy boulder, but that it was officially sealed and guarded by soldiers. This was done out of concern that the disciples might steal the body and perpetrate a hoax. Nevertheless, Matthew notes that even in his day, probably in the AD 80s, there was a persistent rumor of grave robbing. In the accounts we dealt with earlier, we saw that the Risen Jesus went out of his way to demonstrate that he was not a ghost, nor was there an issue of mistaken identity. The evangelists are as aware as we are that resurrection is not easily explained or comprehended; resurrection was not on the horizon of the early disciples as they tried to make sense of what had happened on Easter morning.

- Thus far I have been assuming a bodily resurrection. That is, the same Jesus who had died on the cross was raised by the power of God, appeared in corporeal form to his disciples, and now lives beyond the dominion of death, beyond the boundaries of time and space. But you have likely already noted in our investigations of the resurrection accounts that the Risen Jesus seemed to be able simply to be present and then not present. Also, even those close to him did not always seem to recognize him at first. St. Paul tackles these unsettling factors in that very important chapter 15 of his first letter to the Corinthians. He adopts a rhetorical device common in his day, the diatribe. For him this term does not denote an angry, haranguing speech, but rather a series of movements in an intellectual argument in which the speaker or writer raises questions and issues and then proceeds to answer them. It goes like this: you say that . . . but I will now show you a better answer. Paul uses this technique with the problem of bodily resurrection. He writes, "But someone will ask, 'How are the dead raised? With what kind of body do they come?'" (1 Cor. 15:35). What follows has always seemed to me to be an example of Paul struggling to make clear what is beyond clarity. And surely this issue is one that defies simple answers. Paul continues by speaking about seeds that are planted. To a person without our current scientific understanding, the act of planting seeds makes it appear that the seeds have died. But later the seeds sprout and grow into wheat or grain. That is, the seed seems to die, but from it appears a living plant. He assumes the reader will catch the analogy with Jesus' death, burial, and resurrection. Paul continues with a new set of analogies. He notes that there are many examples of various kinds of entities—human flesh and the flesh of birds, heavenly bodies, and earthly bodies. Again we need to remember that neither Paul nor his readers functioned with a modern, scientific mindset. Maybe the simplest way to state what Paul is thinking is this: things can be placed into distinct categories. But finally he pulls together these two sets of analogies:

> So it is with the resurrection of the dead. What is sown is perishable, what is raised is imperishable. It is sown in dishonor, it is raised in glory. It is sown in weakness, it is raised in power. It is sown a physical body, it is raised a spiritual body. (1 Cor. 15:42–44)

St. Paul understands that the Risen Christ appeared in a body, but in a glorified body, a category of corporeality never seen before. Paul resists the temptation to say more or to explain the unexplainable. For him the sets of analogies he presents offer enough insight to be intellectually satisfying. The most we can say is that this is a mystery. The crucified Jesus is the Risen Christ. And the Risen Christ was actually and corporeally present, but in a way beyond our current understanding.

- Five, many of us were taught to interpret the Bible with "hermeneutic of skepticism." Hermeneutics is the process of trying to determine what the original writers of the Bible said, and what they meant to the people of their own time and to us. In short, it is the process of interpretation of ancient documents. We learned that a variety of intellectual and cultural assumptions demanded that we approach the scriptures with skepticism, with a sense that we were not necessarily dealing with history in a strict sense, but in narratives that contained a bit of wisdom about God or life. The resurrection seemed to be a favorite target of this hermeneutic. The approach was this: since we cannot explain resurrection and can find no other instances of it in the world's literature, then clearly it did not happen. Rather, this approach said, the accounts are narratives that reflect an inner change in the thinking of the disciples without reference to objective reality. In more recent times there has been a serious questioning of this approach, noting that it is based on the assumption that our own, modern understanding are the measure of all things. Today many are coming to say that while the resurrection is a surprising and difficult phenomenon, it is, nevertheless, the only interpretation that adequately addresses both the texts as they stand, and that can account for the utter transformation in thinking and action demonstrated by those early disciples.

- So we can come to a conclusion about this second step in our analysis of resurrection. We can say that resurrection is beyond our comprehension, but that nothing else can adequately account for the resurrection narratives in the New Testament and for the rise of the church.

Our third step seeks to clarify our understanding of the category of miracle. We need to do this first because the resurrection is the miracle par excellence, and second because the whole business of the "miraculous" is a stumbling block for some. The late Professor Reginald Fuller makes very helpful distinctions in his now out-of-print book, *Interpreting the Miracles*. He makes three points:

- He defines a miracle as an event that is contrary to what we currently know. Fuller rightly emphasizes that some miracles may be explainable in the future.
- He notes that miracles are signs, not proofs.
- He says that miracles point beyond themselves to some further meaning. In the scriptures, miracles point to the divine, and ask us to ponder how and why God acts in human history.

Over the years I have turned to Fuller's book again and again. The term I would use to summarize his arguments is "mystery." Miracles in general and resurrection in particular are mysteries in the best sense of that rich word. They are events that we cannot now fully explain, but rather that invite us to explore, to probe, to wonder, even though we may never be able to come to a complete understanding or explanation. Miracles call forth in us thoughts, questions, prayer—and doubt. We stand before the mystery of the resurrection, lost in wonder, doubt, hope, belief, prayer, and worship.

We have come to the end of our three-step journey. If you sensed that we were walking around the edge of the issue of doubt rather than addressing it directly, you are correct. Over the years that I have been thinking and preaching about the resurrection, I have had to come to terms with my own uncertainty. Those very doubts, however, have served to drive me into considering the resurrection texts in a detailed way, to ponder the category of resurrection and to try to untangle the intellectual knots regarding miracles. These pursuits, in turn, have strengthened my faith and my appreciation of the place of doubt in the life of Christians.

In the end we have to say that we bring both doubt and faith along with us in our journey. I do not see how we can disconnect the two, so that we can cast doubt away and cling only to faith.

Faith and doubt are in a continual dialog, a dialog that goes on for the length of our journey in life. Individuals need to relax about their doubts, and accept it as a factor of faith. And churches need to acknowledge that doubt is simply part of any authentic journey with and to the Risen Christ. To put it another way, to shut the door on genuine doubt is to shut the door on genuine faith.

In the New Testament, faith is understood as a gift. We cannot try hard and produce belief. We cannot be so persuasive that we are able to convince everyone to walk with the Risen One. Belief and conversion, rather, are the results of the Risen Lord acting in our lives. Only the Risen One can give us faith, and only the Risen One can convert people. That reality is a further reason, therefore, for us not to beat up on ourselves when doubt creeps in. In fact, doubt may be a corollary of Christ being present and at work in our lives and churches. That is why I say I believe in doubt.

When the proclamation of the resurrection poses doubts and causes us to waver, I suggest the following steps:

First, assume the resurrection and the presence of the Risen Lord are true. We cannot offer ironclad proof for it, but we can experiment, so to speak, with it. Postulate that Christ is risen, and see what happens.

Second, assume it is true, and act accordingly. Base your attitudes, imaginings, and actions on the reality of the Paschal Mystery. Trust that the Risen Christ will bring life out of death at all times and in all ways in your life. If you don't believe it, at least pretend that it is true and go from there.

Third, be aware of what is happening to you as a person and as a church. I sometimes see people floating down one of Montana's beautiful rivers, but they are floating with their eyes shut, apparently asleep. I wonder what the point of a float trip is if you sleep your way through it.

Rather, look for and expect to see signs and hints of the presence of Christ. My testimony is that when you do this, you will clearly perceive the presence of Christ, always available to us and always seeking to bless us.

Questions to Help You Digest this Chapter on Doubt

1. Above I described a three-step process for living with doubt. Can you find instances in your life or in the life of your congregation where this might be a helpful exercise? Give particular instances of what this might look like in action.

2. What are your persistent doubts about God?

3. In what ways might your doubts cause you to deepen your faith? What actions or changes might need to take place?

4. In your reading and discussion of this chapter, what might the Risen Lord be saying to you and be asking you to change?

chapter 7

The Big D and little d's

Not long after I had become bishop, I was called upon to perform a sad and painful duty. One of our small congregations had written a letter asking that their church be closed. They noted that they now consisted of only four members, that they could no longer pay utility bills, that they could see no promising prospects for the near future, and that they had simply run out of energy. I had met with these people several times prior to receiving this letter. I knew that they had a nice building in a good location, and that they individually were good and faithful people. I also learned, however, about a series of events that had resulted in their present circumstance.

We have no official liturgy for the closing of a congregation, but a service for the secularization of a church building is authorized. I made the journey to preside at that liturgy, which would be the last Eucharist in that place. At the time of the sermon, I made some comments that reflected both the scriptures appointed and the occasion of the closing of the parish, and then I asked those present if they had things they wanted to say. What followed was an extended series of stories, tears, regrets, remembrances of times when they had thrived, fears about the future of their spiritual lives, and even some self-blame. The mood was simple sadness; nothing more could be said. It felt to me exactly like a wake for a family member. I heard and felt death, the death of a congregation.

Death is the great fact of life. I remember first learning about entropy in science class. Entropy is the phenomenon of everything in the universe running out of energy, winding down, dying, and I left the classroom that day haunted by the concept. Even at the largest level we can imagine, death operates, provoking fear. That response is natural, of course; we have hopes and inklings about what may or may not lie beyond death, but there is no process by which we know with any certainty about life beyond death. Death is such a slap in the face of life that fear, along with anger and rage, takes hold of our hearts. Humans are such complex, interesting beings, capable of both God-like accomplishments and hellish destruction. The cosmos throbs with activity, beauty, and complexity. And then death arrives at times and in ways unexpected. It denies the thrill of being alive. It can feel as if everything we know and accomplish becomes trash dumped into a dark, bottomless pit.

Little wonder we dance around the fact of mortality. It is such an intense and serious issue that we try to paper over it, ignore it, pretend it is not there. And we even develop euphemisms to pacify our fear and anger: "They are better off. It must be the will of God. They lived a good life." Perhaps, but death still wins.

But before the event of death, the big D, we all experiences many small deaths, little d's. These little d's happen as events and people drain the life out of us, so that we die a little on the inside. Anything that saps hope, joy, accomplishment, a sense of worth, healthy relationships, a firm trust in God is a little d.

We know that our personal stories are replete with instances. There have been the offers of friendship rejected, or professional disappointments. There are failed marriages, domestic violence, soured relations with family and friends. The messengers of little d's are parents who do not care, poor teachers, friends who are jealous, employers who watch only the bottom line. And we must put poverty, injustice, and illness on the list. We all know people and circumstances that simply sap the vitality out of us.

Churches have little d's, too. Church fights are a nearly guaranteed way to introduce death into a parish. Fears about money and loss of members, gossip, lackadaisical involvement, lack of commitment to Christ, no sense of direction—these all open the door to death, which is always ready to enter.

For many folks, death is the end of the story. The movie of life rolls on, "The End" appears on the screen, and soon the theatre is dark and quiet. The book is closed. The well runs dry. Darkness falls. Death.

But with God, death is not the end of the story. Easter bursts forth as the great surprise and the grand reversal of all that we think and know about life. We might well react to the proclamation of the resurrection with "if it's too good to be true, it probably is." Remember in Luke's gospel, for example, that the first reaction of the apostles when they heard the report of an empty tomb and an angelic message of resurrection was to label the story of the women "pure nonsense." That we understand. Nevertheless, the consistent and powerful Easter proclamation is:

- The tomb of Jesus is empty.
- Hundreds of disciples of Jesus were encountered by the Risen Christ.
- And the church today continues to experience the life-changing presence of its Risen Lord.

The message of the two angelic beings in Luke is a powerful summary of what Easter proclaims: "Why do you look for the living among the dead? He is not here, but has risen" (Luke 24:5).

The resurrection is the grandest reversal and the greatest surprise in the human story. Death is not the last word of life, despite evidence to the contrary. God authored the surprise and reversal; God intervened in the person of Jesus, and set in motion the victory of life and the death of death. What at first appears to be nonsense is, in fact, *the* great fact of life.

From the startling and astonishing proclamation of the resurrection of our Lord follow four implications. Let's pursue and explore them.

First, Easter and resurrection are about Jesus. We tend to think the point of Easter is eternal life for us. While that is a legitimate aspect of Easter, the resurrection is the main event in the New Testament, and Jesus, not us, is the focus. When we understand the resurrection as primarily Christological, Easter pronounces that God had vindicated the ministry, suffering, and death of Jesus. It functions as a way of saying God approves of and stands beside what Jesus did.

Not only is the resurrection a sign of vindication, but it is also the victory of Jesus over death and all else that separates us from God. On the cross Christ engaged the enemies—death and sin—in their most virulent form, and on Easter he demonstrated that God conquered those forces. At this point in our discussion, I believe it is helpful to define sin as anything that counters our relationship with God and the blessings God wishes to bestow. Sin functions not only in what each person does or fails to do in thought, word, and deed, but also in anything that influences us to walk away from God. Our innate tendency to place ourselves at the center of our personal universe destroys our connection with divine life and love. But poverty and injustice also work that way in the lives of many people, and in that sense we can label them as sinful. In the resurrection God has acted so decisively that the big D and the little d's are destroyed. Nothing—nothing at all—can stand in the way of God reaching out to embrace us in resurrection life.

Perhaps the most graphic of the few instances in Western art where Jesus is depicted in the act of rising from the grave is a part of the Isenheim Altarpiece painted by Matthias Grünewald in about 1510–1515. It was intended to stand behind the altar of a chapel in a hospital dedicated to the care of people with leprosy and other serious skin diseases. It takes the form of a triptych, a painting on three panels that are attached to each other in such a way that it can be opened or closed. The left-hand panel portrays the Annunciation, the announcement to the Blessed Virgin Mary that she was to be the mother of Jesus. The middle panel is an almost overwhelming portrayal of the crucifixion. The right-hand panel deals with our subject, the resurrection. It shows Jesus in midair, almost as if he had been shot out of the white sepulcher at the bottom of the scene. The sky is pitch black. Jesus himself, however, is wrapped in white, painted in such a way as to make it appear to glow. The usual solemn-faced portrayal of our Lord is changed to a slight smile. In his right hand is a flag of victory. It, too, is gleaming white with a blood red cross in the middle. Everything about this painting says Victory, light over darkness, victory over defeat, life over death. For my money, this stunning painting captures Easter. This image reminds us that Easter is first of all about Jesus and his victory.

The second implication of the resurrection worthy of our investigation is this: God is willing to share the resurrection event with us. Easter begins with Jesus, but soon we are invited into the realm of light, victory, and life. The primary sign and guarantee of our participation in the new creation is baptism. Paul in his letter to the church in Rome (written about AD 57) succinctly makes the connection between resurrection and baptism. He writes:

> Do you not know that all of us who have been baptized into Christ Jesus were baptized into his death? Therefore we have been buried with him by baptism into death, so that, just as Christ was raised from the dead by the glory of the Father, so we too might walk in newness of life. For if we have been united with him in a death like his, we will certainly be united with him in a resurrection like his. (Rom. 6:3–5)

Note carefully the phrase "baptized into Christ Jesus." Paul understands baptism as an act of God on behalf of and for the benefit of the baptismal candidate. God joins the baptized to the Risen One. This suggests that the pattern of Jesus' story of death to life will be the pattern by which God works in the life of the baptized. Jesus' story becomes our story.

The impact of baptism is probably best symbolized by total immersion, a method of baptism in which the candidate is dunked completely under water—totally immersed—and then pulled up out of the water. This is not to say that other forms of baptism are not valid; all I am suggesting is that immersion "paints the picture" vividly. Being placed under the water suggests death and burial. I knew a seminary professor who only half-jokingly said that if you were baptizing a person this way, you should hold them under the water until they turned blue. Well, that would convey the horror and threat of death, but I would not suggest that that represents good pastoral judgment! Then the person is pulled out of the water by the priest, suggesting life and resurrection. The point is that in baptism God shares the resurrection with us. God promises to be at work in and among, bringing resurrection and life.

The third implication proclaims that nothing can separate us from the love of God. If God can deal with death, I think that proves that God can deal with anything, any sin that injures our relationship with God and any power that draws us away from God. Again in the letter to the Romans, Paul summarizes it well. Some people think of Paul merely as an overly serious theologian whose writings are challenging to understand. But Paul was more than that; Paul could be, when inspired, a poet equal to any you can think of. For instance, Paul's rhapsody about love in 1 Corinthians 13 is so moving that it is read at nearly every wedding I have ever attended or officiated. In Romans 8, Paul is moved to soaring heights as he thinks about the love and the victory of Christ.

> What then are we to say about these things? If God is for us, who is against us? He who did not withhold his own Son, but gave him up for all of us, will he not with him also give us everything else? . . . Who will separate us from the love of Christ? Will hardship, or distress, or persecution, or famine, or nakedness, or peril, or sword? . . . I am convinced that neither death, nor life, nor angels, nor rulers, nor things present, nor things to come, nor powers, nor height, nor depth, nor anything else in all creation, will be able to separate us from the love of God in Christ Jesus our Lord. (Rom. 8:31–32, 35, 38–39)

The love of God revealed in the resurrection inspired Paul to this flight of inspiration. I confess that this text inspires in me greater love for God and more confidence in the resurrection, so much so that I have asked that this passage be read at my funeral.

The fourth implication can be stated in one word: hope. This virtue and gift (and in the New Testament it is both) is essentially a way of looking at the future. Resurrection says to us that we can face any circumstance with a confidence that God will be operating according to the pattern of the Paschal Mystery, making life out of death. Further, God operates this way for us and our benefit. Resurrection is not a foggy concept that floats up there in our mental atmosphere. The resurrection is *for us*.

We need to add that hope is a very important factor in the life of people and of parishes. Hope engenders energy, confidence, and a sense of worth about our lives and ministries. In sharing the lives of people as a priest for three decades, I observed that people with hope can endure almost anything with grace and even humor. The Resurrected Lord creates hope in our hearts.

We hear a lot today about the word "evangelical." As used by the secular press, it refers to a certain kind of piety and outlook inculcated in a certain kind of church. The word has frankly been hijacked and misused. It is a very positive concept, and every Christian and every church should seek to be evangelical, just as they should seek to be catholic, another hijacked term. The word evangelical actually has this history. It is based in a Greek word *euangelion,* a term frequently used in the New Testament. The *eu* is a positive prefix, suggesting something desirable and good. The *angelion* part of the word simply means a message or a report. This enters English as the word evangel, which essentially means good news. Indeed, the New Testament evangel denotes THE good news of the gospel of Jesus Christ, crucified and raised. The word is made even richer when we consider that in the common everyday Greek of the first century, the word was often used to refer to the public announcement of victory over enemies. It denotes front-page news with a bold print headline: WE WON. For Christians it reads: HE WON. WE WIN. To be evangelical is to center ourselves in the resurrection. What better news is there?

By this time I hope you see that the resurrection is God's direct and positive response to the issue of death in all its form. Many factors in our lives suggest that death conquers all, but the resurrection counters that in a profound and universal way. Life conquers. Love wins. The Risen Christ is the victor. I was recently wandering through a seminary bookstore and noted that a systematic theology class was reading *Christus Victor* by the Swedish bishop Gustaf Aulén. It was first published in the 1930s, but even seventy years later it is still in print, and I never fail to find it in seminary bookstores and on reading lists. Aulén's point is that the victory of Jesus in the resurrection is the very heart of the message of the New Testament. We would radically miss the point, he says, if we do not understand this. God in Christ conquers. God has responded to our cries of anguish about both the big D and little d's, and that response takes the form of Easter, resurrection, the victory of divine like and love. Christus victor.

Given the evangel of Christ's resurrection and our baptismal initiation into the resurrection, how do we choose to live? How do we put that good news into action in church and in our lives? The resurrection will have little or no power for us if we do not let it loose in our lives. As I have suggested earlier, awareness and attitude stand as key components in the challenge of living the resurrection. All of us need to develop the discipline to be conscious of and open to what goes on around us. We cannot simply limp along with mouth gaping and eyes staring at the ground. Awareness, in turn, is based on attitude. We can train our minds and imaginations to be resurrectional. We can structure our thinking so that resurrection is in the forefront of our thinking.

I recently watched a snippet of an interview with a woman who writes cookbooks. She was asked about where her recipes come from. With a smile she said, "I love to cook and try new foods. So I watch for new dishes, and I ask people and chefs for their recipes. I find them wherever I go." She had developed an attitude and receptivity for recipes. And that was linked to her obvious joy in new tastes and smells. Similarly, wherever we go, we can develop a resurrection awareness and attitude.

To help with this discipline, consider these Ten Commandments of Resurrectional Thinking. They apply both to persons and congregations.

1. Always expect the presence of the Risen Christ. Assume that he will be present. Just as you expect and trust that breathing in will fill your lungs, so expect that Jesus will seek you out and be present.

2. Never forget that you are baptized. To state it another way, know who you are. Know your identity. There is a story about Martin Luther, perhaps apocryphal, that when he was sorely tempted, he would grab a piece of chalk and write in

large letters on the top of a wooden table: "I am baptized." I suppose all of us can easily recall examples of when we have lost sight of our best selves, our baptismal identity, and have quickly gone off the rails.

3. Assume that Christ will be present without regard to what you feel. One of the major issues of religion in our country is our tendency to think of religion in terms of feelings, that religion is real, is validated, only by religious feelings. The problem is that our feelings are not accurate gauges of the presence of the Risen One; our feelings are accurate gauges only of our feelings. You may feel nothing; do not conclude that Jesus is not there. You may feel so overwhelmed by death that you want to opt out of this whole resurrection business; do not assume that Jesus will not use you as an agent of resurrection anyway. You feel depressed and despairing; do not think that means Jesus has left the room or that you are being punished for something. And for goodness sake, do not judge your church or your priest by their ability to manufacture in you a religious high. God can do his best work when we feel nothing. Moreover, we need God the most exactly at those times when we feel the worst.

4. Be open to the possibility that even you and even your church can be touched by the Risen One. I notice that many people simply conclude that being transformed by Jesus or being an agent of resurrection is for someone else who is smarter, knows their Bible better, lives a more disciplined life, has been a church member longer, and so forth. And I have also noticed the tendency of church people to think that the church down the street is better than their own congregation. They think they know examples of vital churches, but they have concluded

that theirs is not or cannot be one of those resurrectional congregations. In the diocese I am privileged to serve, I can tell you that every single congregation, large and small, rural and urban, has at least one significant resurrectional ministry going on, and many have multiple examples of this. It could be you and your church where the Risen Christ lives. In fact, you can count on it.

5. Plan on the Risen Christ shaking up things. We are asked to alter aspects of our life or that of our church whenever Christ encounters us. Just read any of the gospels, and you will find ample proof that wherever Jesus went, controversy would follow. The problem is that most of us do not like change, and what we prefer is the status quo we know, understand, and can control. When I am asked by leaders of congregations what they can do to grow and be more vital, my first response is usually a question: how much are you willing to change? When Jesus is at hand, expect that he will rattle the cage. For those of us who are middle-class Americans, you can be sure that he will want to shake you in two areas: what you do with your money, and how you respond to the needs of the poor and marginalized. We tend to want to reply, the money I earn is mine, and the poor can get to work and earn their own. From Jesus' perspective, we are only stewards of the gifts he gives, and that includes our money and our ability to earn it. And Jesus may choose to be present with the poor and the marginalized through us. You will need to fasten your seat belts when Jesus is at hand; there will be turbulence ahead.

6. The Risen Lord will provide what we need. This is one of the most difficult aspects of resurrectional living appropriate both

for people and for parishes. Rather, we tend to operate on the scarcity model: we have to cut, we have to pull back, we have to reduce, because we do not have enough money, people, time, money, energy, talent, money, savings, and money to do what the Lord needs us to do. I was once interviewing at a church as a candidate to be their rector. I asked, "How do you make decisions?" One Vestry member without a moment's hesitation said, "We see if we have enough money." Certainly we are called to be good and faithful stewards of what we have, but I think that man had it upside-down. We begin with the question of mission: what is Christ calling us to do? The question of resources comes further down the list, and we need to learn to trust that the Risen Lord will provide enough to do what he calls us to do.

7. "Being realistic" may not be realistic. I wish I had a dollar for every time I have heard someone say, "We have to be realistic." What usually—not always—but usually follows is a way to side-step mission, service, and the need to relinquish our sense of control over power and turf. We are most realistic when we are confident in the Risen Lord and less certain about our perception of our limitations.

8. The Risen Christ can overcome any issue. This is a simple and prosaic way of stating what Paul said in the Romans 8 passage. There is nothing that our Lord is not able to cope with and transform—even our hearts. One of the members of the diocesan staff has a little plaque on her desk that reads: "The impossible takes longer." Remember, Christ is the Victor.

9. Learn to recognize the pattern of the Paschal Mystery. When Christ is active, death in any form will be turned to

life following the pattern of the resurrection. We live by our ability to recognize patterns. For instance, we have learned the patterns of driving on an interstate highway, of shopping in a huge supermarket, of handling forms and applications, of having a bank account. We know how to go about these activities because we have mastered the patterns. If we are to make our way through our life's journey, it is simply absolutely imperative that we recognize the pattern by which the Risen Lord operates.

10. Think big. The resurrection itself is a stunning instance of how big God can think. Again, thinking big requires that we let go of some of our usual assumptions about limits and expectations. I have previously mentioned the first Bishop of Montana, Daniel Tuttle. He was elected at age 29 by the House of Bishops to become the first missionary bishop of what they termed the Diocese of Montana. In fact, that missionary district was composed of Montana, Idaho, and Utah. Someone in the House of Bishops was thinking big. And Tuttle stepped up to the challenge, because he was thinking big.

We spend so much of our time and energy dealing with the inevitability of all the forms of death. It is a waste of those precious commodities, because Christ is risen. Let's get on with living the resurrection.

Questions to Help Clarify Your Understanding of Death and Resurrection

1. In one simple sentence, are you able to define the "Paschal Mystery"?

2. Can you describe an important moment in your life where the Risen Christ was active in resurrectional ways?

3. Where is resurrection happening in your church?

4. What places in your life and in your church do you need to pray for a resurrection?

IMPLICATIONS

I grew up within sight and earshot of the Ohio River, one of the great waterways of America. It held a large place in my imagination and self-awareness, and it commanded physical attention for those of us living around it. On summer days I understood it as a place of recreation and pleasure. As I thought about earning money, I saw towboats pulling huge barges full of goods. I learned that they could be dangerous. From these facts about the river that loomed so large in my imagination, I drew implications. For example, since is was a recreational asset, that implied that I could swim in it or go on boat rides; I did both of those things. It was profitable, and I concluded that if I had been interested, I could have earned a living on a towboat or constructing bridges. Because it was dangerous, I took care never to swim alone.

In this second part of our exploration of living in the resurrection, we will look at implications of living as a disciple of the Risen Lord. In the first part we looked at resurrectional responses to human issues, and I hope, as a result, Easter began to loom large in your imagination and understanding. Now we will take the "fact-ness" of the resurrection and spin out from it how it might affect the way we live and how it might call us to change our behavior both as persons and as part of the church, the community of the resurrection.

If a group of Easter people, persons whose understanding and imaginations were filled with resurrection awareness, were to sit down and brainstorm about the implications of the resurrection of our Lord, I am certain they could develop a list with scores of items. I, however, have not tried to test myself to see how many implications I could record. Rather, I looked to my experience as the chief shepherd of a specific portion of Christ's flock, and with that flock in mind, I have chosen a small list of implications that arise from working with them. We Montanans like to think of ourselves as unique, but I trust not so unique that my thoughts will not be helpful to others.

chapter 8

We Gather Together

I have relatives who claim no association with any church. They also appear to be uncomfortable around those of us in the family who are serious members of a congregation. In the course of any discussion about a church in particular or religion in general, this refrain often appears: "I feel closer to God by taking a walk in the woods than in going to church."

Over the years of ordained ministry, I have heard variations on that theme many times. And I feel some sympathy for the sentiment. A walk in the woods often produces a sense of calm and wonder in me, too. And I also have to admit that some congregations can wear you out with their trivial pursuits and silly conflicts. But the comment continues to bother me. I have fantasized saying in response, "Fine. But do the trees have good news for you? Do the squirrels administer the sacraments to you? Do the clouds offer the comfort and challenge your deepest self needs?" I have never actually spoken those thoughts, because I know sarcasm seldom promotes the work of God. What I am attempting to say is this: a walk in the woods is not resurrectional.

The comments of my relatives manifest some of the attitudes of our culture about religion, and these attitudes have become so basic that we seldom give them a critical look or are even aware of their influence. I believe our culture functions with a view of religion that has three components.

First, religion is an individual affair. We tend to assume that a person's faith is personal and private, so much so that someone's belief cannot be questioned or evaluated. "It's what they believe," we say with a shrug. For example, we have a segment of our culture that believes in astrology, and they seek to shape their lives according to the movements and alignments of the stars and planets. It is an ancient belief, astrology, based on the idea that the stars and planets are demigods whose divine powers influence the course of human affairs. Of course, no one thinks that planets and stars are demigods, and the only force they have is gravity. Yet astrology persists, and no one feels they are right to challenge this belief system. After all, religion is personal and private.

Second, religion focuses on the soul. The thinking runs this way. Everyone has a soul, that little spark of the divine, and, if we do the right things, the soul will go to heaven when we die. This approach does not take into account the body, the mind, the will, or the imagination. Indeed, it does not take into account anything physical or corporeal. If we discuss the nature of soul, we soon encounter serious problems, the chief ones being where and what the soul is. There is a story, perhaps true, perhaps not, that the great seventeenth century thinker René Descartes became intrigued by the concept of the human soul, and this interest provoked him to develop an experiment. The story says that he put people who were near death on scales. When they died, he hoped to show a difference in the weight of the body, which he postulated would be proof of the soul. He was never able to find a difference in the before and after weights. I am not trying to malign Descartes, often called the father of modern philosophy and a brilliant mathematician. I do think, however, that this story indicates how deeply we are interested in the idea of a soul, and how much faith we are willing to invest in it.

Third, religion is emotional. As noted previously, our culture thinks and talks about religion in terms of feelings, assumes that real religion is emotional, and validates religion on the basis of whether or not it produces certain feelings. As I listen to the culture, I hear that a sense of uplift and inspiration, feelings of confidence, and in some circles even ecstasy are signs that you are dealing with the genuine article. The reasons for this are rooted in nineteenth century philosophy and certain aspects of eighteenth century church life in America. But whatever its roots, real religion is understood to be emotional religion.

These factors are constitutive of our American religion: private, soul focused, and emotionally validated. So pervasive are these that almost all of us assume them as part of our views of faith and belief.

We are now in a place where we can listen to a resurrection story that directly addresses our situation. We return again to the gospel according to John (John 20:19–23). We have already explored this text, but let's do a quick review of it. The disciples have locked themselves in a room on Easter evening, because they feared arrest from the religious authorities. The Risen Christ appears, greets them with the words "Peace be with you," shows them his hands and side. Again he gifts them with the Holy Spirit and sends them forth to continue his ministry. I find five just-below-the-surface elements that address our situation.

First, note that the account focuses on the gathered community, not on individuals. Christ is present among them, not in individuals. Indeed, with the exception of Thomas, no individuals' names are listed. The gathered community is locus of the narrative.

Second, Jesus centers his attention on the community, and its ministry and identity. Indeed, the church is the focus of the rest of the New Testament as well. The scriptural terms often translated as "church" are *ekklesia* and *koinonia*. The first literally means the people who are called out; the phrase "chosen people" is not off the mark. *Koinonia* is based on the idea of commonality, a group of people with something in common; the church is this sort of community in a profound way. This passage from John, then, tells us that the church is where the Risen Christ is present and through which the Risen One has promised to work. No doubt, Christ can and does work elsewhere, but the community of those called by Jesus is the arena in which he has promised that he can be found.

Third, Jesus' gift of peace plays an important role in the good news of the resurrection. In the text, Christ twice gives the gift of peace, suggesting it is a necessary element in the identity and ministry of the resurrection community. Peace here should not be understood merely as the absence of conflict. In the terminology of John's gospel, "peace" and "abundant life" are closely allied. Living the resurrection is nearly synonymous with living the abundant life Jesus promised, and peace is a primary, basic ingredient. When God's plan comes together, peace results. So, it is no accident that on the day of resurrection, the first word of Jesus to his disciples is peace. In the resurrection, the plan of God comes together. And we all love it when a plan comes together.

Fourth, to the embryo church locked away in that room, Christ makes himself present and gives the Holy Spirit. As we have noted, the Holy Spirit is invisible yet real, everywhere and always present among the followers of the Risen One. Observe carefully that the Spirit is given to the community, the church.

Fifth, Jesus gives his community a charter, a purpose, a reason for being. Our Lord has chosen us, formed us into a community, and has asked us to take up where he left off in his earthly ministry. The Risen One calls us to live in the resurrection in such a way that we become agents of resurrection, ambassadors of new life, activists for abundant living. This book began with a meditation on the Garden of Eden as a symbol of the peace, blessing, and community which God wants for the whole cosmos. In John's gospel, the first person to meet the Risen One was Mary Magdalene—in a garden. She mistakes Jesus for the gardener. He is, in fact, God's gardener, working through us to grow a new garden, a new world, characterized by concord, life lived to the full, and community. Jesus has given us a mission.

I hope you sense that the cultural view of religion stands in stark contrast to the religion of the resurrection. Life in the new creation is shared with others, is concerned with the total entities of human beings and the environment, and is oriented toward mission and ministry.

I am responsible for writing pastoral letters. These are official statements from the bishop about some important topic, and canon law requires that they be read in churches. If I were to write a pastoral letter about the most important and timely of topics, the resurrection, I would lift up and celebrate three implications of Easter.

First, you cannot be saved alone. The resurrection life is never personal, private, or individualistic. For instance, a person cannot baptize herself; it is an act that must involve at least two persons. A person cannot celebrate the Eucharist by himself; it must involve at least two persons. The Bible was produced by the people of God and is intended to be used by the people of God; private interpretations do not suffice. Further, all of us who attempt to follow the Risen Lord do that as a result of the words and actions of others. In my own cast, parents and grandparents, priests and Sunday school teachers, authors of books, and painters of pictures have all pushed and pulled me toward Jesus.

Second, you must participate in the life of the church. Long ago I took part in training for personal evangelism. In part, I was required to tell my God story, my journey with God. I also practiced listening to the stories of a number of laypersons from the churches in the area. A major point of learning from those latter conversations was that for most people there is no distinction between their God story and their participation in the church. At first that disturbed me, but I began to recognize the truth of their witness. The church is the community where we encounter and are encountered by the Risen One. To talk about knowing Jesus is to mention all those people who have been his voice and hands.

I recognize that asking people to be part of an intentional and sometimes intense community of resurrection is no easy matter. Others irritate, others inflict hurt, others insist on accountability, so much so that we long to believe we do not need the church and that we can go it alone. As a result, a particular temptation of our busy and tiring lives is to skip Sunday Eucharist, to simply sidestep the whole affair. I admit that even I sometimes have visions of a quiet Sunday morning with the paper and a pot of tea. To counter this enticement, we should remember that we need to feast on the Body and Blood of our Lord, we need to hear scripture read and preached, we need the simple encouragement of seeing other

Christians, and they need to see us, too. Regular attendance may not be convenient, but it is, nevertheless, essential.

Third, the church needs to be seized by a sense of mission. As we have said again and again, the resurrection impels us to take up the work that our Lord has given us, the work of sharing in nothing less than the redemption of the universe. The church does not exist to comfort just the groups that gather under its various roofs, and certainly it does not exist to make me comfortable. We exist to glorify the Risen One, to mature in our relationship with Christ, and to go out and do his work.

Every congregation should seek to be clear about its identity and its mission. Every church should be able to state in a single, simple sentence what they believe Christ to be calling them to do, given their unique gifts, history, and location. This, however, is easier said than done. Some congregations try to do it in a weekend Vestry retreat, and that is a good start—but it is only a start. I believe the place to begin is for the people of the church to pledge themselves to six months of intentional prayer about their mission and six months of scripture study. Then we wait, quiet ourselves, and listen. Christ will make clear his call.

That would be the contents of my imaginary pastoral letter. We are in this together, not alone. We need to be together as an intentional community of resurrection. And we should be clear and certain about our mission.

Years ago I was introduced to the African Bible Study Method; some call it the Cell Method—"cell" referring to a small group of people—or the Lambeth Method, because it was introduced at a Lambeth Conference of Anglican Bishops. The directions for conducting it vary a bit according to which source you read, but it usually follows this plan:

- The group gathers, and a passage of scripture is chosen. Many groups use one of the readings appointed for use in the previous or approaching Sunday. A group member offers a short prayer inviting the presence and guidance of the Risen Lord.

- The members sit in a circle and are asked to listen especially to the comments of the person to their right.

- The scripture passage is read aloud slowly by two different people, preferably one male voice and one female voice.

- Silence follows.

- In turn each person tells the group what word or phrase caught their attention. At this point and at any other points, any person may choose not to speak.

- The passage is read again, preferably in another translation. And again, silence follows.

- Each person in the group then answers this question: What word or phrase has touched my life and why?

- A third time the passage is read, again in another translation. Silence follows.

- Each person responds to these questions: On the basis of what I have read and heard, what is God seeking to say to me now? What is God asking me to change now?

- Finally, the session ends with prayer, with each person praying for the one sitting to their right.

As you see, this is striking in its simplicity and does not require someone with expertise in the Bible. I have participated in this method dozens of times, and I can testify that it has always been a time of blessing. I have never left without a sense of being heard by others and without a sense that God has spoken to me.

This study method stands as a compelling example of power and importance of living the resurrection by living in the community of the church. We need each other in order to persevere in our journey of faith. We are called to be faithful, active members of a congregation, for to fail to do so would imperil our relationship with God. As difficult as life in a parish can be, nothing can substitute for it.

I have titled this chapter after a hymn we often associate with Thanksgiving, "We gather together to ask the Lord's blessing." The author is anonymous, but we know that it was written in the seventeenth century. The life of the church is the theme of the hymn.

Beside us to guide us, our God with us joining,
Ordaining, maintaining his kingdom divine;
So from the beginning the fight we were winning;
Thou, Lord, wast at our side: all glory be thine!
(The Hymnal 1982, number 433)

This hymn sings a song to the Risen Lord, the one always available and blessing the instrument of the resurrection in the world, the church. We are the resurrection people who gather together around our victorious Lord.

Questions for a Group to Engender an Experience of Being Church

1. What are the positive and negative connotations of the word "church" for you?

2. What do you value most in the people of your congregation?

3. In The Episcopal Church and in all catholic churches, the diocese is considered the basic unit of the church. How does your diocese assist you in being a resurrection community?

4. What do you need to change in your life to help you be a resurrection person in your church and diocese?

chapter 9

Worship Is Good for You

I n this country we have little contact with the 1662 *Book of Common Prayer* of the Church of England. While that church has authorized many worship materials in contemporary language, the 1662 prayer book still stands as the official BCP in England and is still used in some parishes. When I read it or hear it, I am always struck both by the elegance of the language and by its old-fashioned quality. One of those moments comes in "The Form of Solemnization of Matrimony." As the groom puts the ring on the finger of the bride, he says, "With this ring I thee wed, with my body I thee worship, and with all my worldly goods I thee endow: In the Name of the Father, and of the Son, and of the Holy Ghost. Amen" (p. 304).

My attention always focuses on the word "worship," because we do not use the term in this particular way today. It surely seems overwrought that the groom states that he will worship his wife. This uncommon usage pulls us back to the underlying and basic concept of "worship." It connotes the idea of giving appropriate value and worth to someone or something that we highly honor and value. The rest of the vow given with the ring fills out this definition. A ring has always been seen as a sign of honor and sometimes of authority. In the marriage ceremony, then, the groom solemnly states that he will give high honor and worth to his bride with his body, with his worldly goods, and with his attitudes and actions. And all of this is symbolized in the gift of a ring, usually fashioned out of valuable material like gold or silver.

We today often use the word "worship" in reference to the activity that a church does on Sunday morning. The American *Book of Common Prayer* says that the Holy Eucharist is "the principal act of Christian worship on the Lord's Day and other major Feasts" (p. 13). As with most things in the prayer book, it must be read with careful attention. Note that Sunday is called the Lord's Day, because we believe this is a time given over to the Lord Jesus Christ. Sunday is the day so set aside, because it was on Sunday, the first day of the week, that the resurrection accounts tell us Christ was raised from the dead. Every Sunday is a little Easter and therefore is considered a major Feast.

Further, what we do on Sunday is Holy Eucharist, that is, Holy Thanksgiving, for that is the meaning of the word "eucharist." All of this is gathered up and presented to God in what the BCP calls "worship."

By the setting aside of time, in considering that time as a special feast in the context of Easter, and by gathering together, we offer God "worship," manifesting our honor and value.

What I wish to highlight is this: worship flows directly from resurrection, and resurrection directly evokes worship. To be a people living the resurrection means we are people who give ourselves over to the worship of the God of the resurrection. We say to God, "Because of what you have done in the resurrection of your Son and our Lord, we kneel before you to respond by giving you our worship, by honoring and valuing you above all else."

The gospels tell us that worship was part of the disciples' response to the Risen One. Here is Luke's account: "While [Jesus] was blessing them, he withdrew from them and was carried up into heaven. And they worshipped him, and returned to Jerusalem with great joy" (Luke 24:51–52).

The climactic scene in this gospel finds the disciples worshipping the Lord. The word the evangelist used for worship suggests the act of kneeling and falling down before someone; this is worship that takes both a physical and mental form.

Matthew's gospel offers another account of this event. Jesus has met the disciples on a mountaintop in Galilee and gives his parting words to the gathered apostles. Note this description: "When they saw [Jesus], they worshipped him" (Matt. 28:17). Again the word used denotes worship in the form of kneeling.

Worship of the Risen One can take an unexpected turn, and again it is Luke's gospel that offers some pointed examples. The little group of women headed up by Mary Magdalene goes to the tomb of Jesus on Sunday morning, and they find the tomb empty. Two angels greet them, and "The women were terrified and bowed their faces to the ground, but the men said to them, 'Why do you look for the living among the dead?'" (Luke 24:5).

On the evening of that same day in Jerusalem, the disciples were talking among themselves about reports of Jesus' appearances. While discussing these events, "Jesus himself stood among them and said to them, 'Peace be with you.' They were startled and terrified" (Luke 24:36–37).

To be in the presence of the divine, these episodes suggest, is to respond with worship but also with fear. These days, fear has a bad rep in the church. Even in confirmation class I can remember being told that when the Bible talks about fearing God, that fear is not really what is meant. I found that confusing, and still do. But this sense of fear in the presence of Christ points to a factor we need to consider.

In his classic book *The Idea of the Holy,* Rudolf Otto analyzes this phenomenon. The phrase he coined to connote religious fear is "mysterium tremendum." He continues by noting that this sort of experience is related to the words awe and awful. It suggests a sense of trembling or shuddering in the "overpowerlingness" of the divine presence. The result is a sense of energy and urgency. The basic point of Otto's book is that this religious fear is a sign that one is in the presence of the living God.

A former parishioner and religion professor took on the project of interviewing a wide variety of people who claimed that they had had a religious experience. He told me that one of the most surprising conclusions was that every single person said their religious experience had an element of *mysterium tremendum.*

The scriptures offer us many examples. The sixth chapter of Isaiah is the prophet's account of a divine encounter in the Jerusalem Temple. His first response is: "Woe is me! I am lost, for I am a man of unclean lips, and I live among a people of unclean lips; yet my eyes have seen the King, the Lord of hosts!" (Isaiah 6:5).

We find this same response in reaction to Jesus. In an episode from the early days of his ministry, Jesus is in a boat on the Sea of Galilee with Peter and others. They go into deep water and spend the night fishing with no success. Jesus tells them to lower their nets—and when they do, they catch so many fish that the nets begin to break. At this, Peter falls on his knees before Jesus, and says, "'Go away from me, Lord, for I am a sinful man!' For he and all who were with him were amazed" (Luke 5:8). Part of the import of this account is that it alerts us early on that Peter recognizes that when he is in the presence of Jesus, he is in the presence of God.

Religious fear, then, serves to validate a religious experience and is concomitant with an encounter with God. Related is the sense that one is sinful, inadequate, unclean in the presence of the One who is holiness itself. Given these factors, we should not be surprised to recognize fear as a part of the resurrection stories.

Nor should we be too quick to dismiss the idea that we should not fear God. It constitutes an essential part of being in the presence of God and indeed marks that experience as a genuine encounter with the divine. The bottom line is that we may well expect that disturbing sense of fear and inadequacy as part of our worship.

This sidebar about worship and fear helps us realize that when we speak of giving honor to the One who is victor even over death, we should not expect that it will always be a nice, comfortable, warm fuzzy experience. Worship is serious business. In that story about Isaiah, he reports that the pivots of the Temple shook. Don't be surprised that in our worship of Christ, things might get shaken up.

The letter to the Colossians contains a moving and poetic passage about our Lord. Some scholars suggest that it may be an early hymn of the church:

> [Christ] is the image of the invisible God, the firstborn of all creation; for in him all things in heaven and on earth were created, things visible and invisible . . . all things have been created through him and for him. He himself is before all things, and in him all things hold together. He is the head of the body, the church; he is the beginning, the firstborn from the dead, so that

he might come to have first place in everything. For in him all the fullness of God was pleased to dwell. (Col. 1:15-19)

We quickly conclude that this is an exalted hymn of praise to Christ, and as such is worship. This poem claims many things for Christ: that he is the icon of God, that through him all things were created, that he is the cohesive power of the universe, and much more. But note that the pivot point in it is that Jesus is the firstborn of the dead. The resurrection is the keyhole through which we look to see the identity of Jesus.

The subject of this hymn-poem is the One whom we worship, and who promises to be present in our worship. The only possible response to such a One is worship—serious, deep, down-on-our-knees awe, fear, joy in our adoration of the Victor. To be with the Risen Lord is to be impelled to worship. Given the resurrection, how can we refuse to give him our highest honor and our highest value?

As we lift up the centrality of worship of the Risen Lord in our faith journey, we might well ask what we can expect in worship. What will happen to us? What should we look for? Expect to experience six factors:

Expect that the Risen Christ will be present. This alone ought to constrain us to be at church. As you may know, the liturgy of The Episcopal Church and many other churches consists of two parts. The first is grandly titled, "The Word of God." There are preliminaries, so to speak, that help us prepare and center ourselves; this is called the Entrance Rite and includes the opening acclamation, the collect for purity, and a song of praise. After that the focus is firmly on the reading of the scriptures, which normally consists of three readings and a psalm, and always consists of at least a reading from one of the gospels. Following on the heels of the reading is the sermon, which seeks to apply the message of the readings to the lives of people today. And then the Creed and the prayers follow.

Beneath this lies the assumption that the Risen Lord will use these elements, especially the readings and the sermon, as a means of speaking to us today. I believe that our Lord has promised to be among us when we gather to worship, and that he will address us if we are quiet enough to listen. Hence, we can hardly overvalue the importance of careful liturgical leadership, careful reading, and careful preaching. These serve as agencies of nothing less than the Word of God.

The second half of the liturgy is called "The Holy Communion," which again suggests that something of solemn importance is about to happen. Gifts of bread, wine, and money are offered; these are blessed in the form of the Eucharistic prayer; the bread is broken; and the consecrated bread and wine are given to the people of the Risen Lord. Again, Christ meets us hidden in the bread and wine, feeding us with his resurrection life and his deathless love. In worship the Risen One speaks to us and shares with us his resurrection life. Therefore, expect Christ to be present at worship.

As an aside, I wonder if we in the church have been assiduous enough in our teaching about worship. So many are lackadaisical about attendance, and some that do attend seem distracted or uninvolved. If we arrived at the church expecting to meet the One whom we worship, love, and value above all else, surely much better attendance and participation would follow.

Second, *expect to find comfort.* We should anticipate that when Christ encounters us, we will find the forgiveness, acceptance, and sense of significance that we all seek. Some years ago I had the opportunity to attend worship at a Melkite Rite Church in the old city of Jerusalem. I was not prepared for what I saw when I walked through the door. Every surface of the church except the floor was covered with bright, well-executed icons. On the walls near congregational eye level, we could look and see ourselves in the company of various saints, confessors, and martyrs. Higher up on the walls were the apostles and the evangelists, then on the ceiling the hosts of heaven. High above the altar was the Blessed Virgin Mary, and above her, larger than any other image, was the Risen Lord sitting on a throne. Though I found it disconcerting that he seemed to be looking directly at me as I was kneeling in my pew, ultimately his right hand, raised in the sign of blessing, was for me an experience of solace on a profound level. Here I was, surrounded by saints above in heaven and my fellow saints below, as well as the great saints and the angels, all of us together worshipping. And there was the Lord, looking at me and giving me his blessings. I sensed deep comfort, the comfort of being near the one I call Lord, who was blessing me with abundant life.

As an aside, note that I say comfort. I am not suggesting that we ought to leave worship necessarily grinning with happiness or feeling like we are floating on a cloud. That might happen, of course, but that is not what I mean by comfort. Rather, we will be met by the One we love, worship, and value above all others, and he will know us, accept us, and bless us even if we feel depressed, lost, overlooked, or unwell. For me that is comfort, indeed.

Third, *expect to be challenged*. We have previously noted that Jesus calls us all to grow up, to mature in our relationship with him. Christ will not let us float mindlessly, half-heartedly on our journey to and with him. He will nudge, tug, and admonish us.

He may step on our existential toes. We always have the right to ignore all of this or simply refuse to do what he asks us. But we dare not think we will escape unchallenged.

As a college freshman I enrolled in a course that was in those days called Western Civilization. It was essentially a class about European and American history. The instructor was not an easy-going person; he was always prepared himself and clearly expected that we would be, too. One assignment was to write a short paper, which I did. When the paper was returned, I had received a mediocre grade, a C as I remember, accompanied by the following comment: "You do not write well." I was furious. In high school I had garnered A's with little effort, including the papers and exams I wrote. As I walked back to my room and as my anger cooled off, I had to admit to myself that he was correct. I did not know exactly what made for good writing, but I was being challenged to become a better student. I didn't like it at first, but I learned through that stark comment on my paper that I needed to find a way to improve my skills.

Expect Jesus to write a blunt comment. Do not expect that you will always get an A. All of us have more work to do.

As an aside, perhaps the biggest challenge is learning to live as community, as a church. Our sisters and brothers in baptism can be the source of exasperation and irritation, and, even more, some of them can be dangerous with their gossip, fault-finding, and power-plays. Many of the former church members I meet have become disillusioned by this and have simply left. The challenge is to see others as the beloved of Christ, as persons with gifts and talents, as resurrection agents who may say or do just what we need to hear or receive. The challenge is to develop the virtues of patience, forbearance, and above all, love, the supreme virtue.

Fourth, *expect to offer yourself to Christ and to his church.* I have found that a sure way to produce confusion and amusement in a church is to use the phrase, "Now we have an opportunity to give." The confused are saying to themselves, "What do you mean by 'opportunity?' I am here to get, not give." And the amused are thinking, "OK, here comes the press for more money." We live in a world governed by materialism. We should understand materialism as a belief system and a way of life; it is a religion without a divinity. It tells us that the name of the game is getting and holding; that what we earn is ours; and that the more we have, the happier we will be. In the long run, materialism does not work, but our society has yet to come to that conclusion. The danger is that we carry alternative religion into worship with us. The measure of genuine worship is not "Did I get something out of it?" And far too many members try to give as little as possible of themselves, believing that who they are and what they have belongs to them.

I can tell what or who a person worships by looking in two places, his or her checkbook and calendar. What we truly worship will show in what and to whom we give. Worship always implies giving—giving to what or whom we love and value. It is not an accident that Christian worship always involves an offering, which usually takes the form of gifts of money. In American society, money is what we receive in return for our time and effort, and it, therefore, represents who we are better than any other commodity. This should neither surprise nor offend us; offering ourselves incorporates an essential component of worship. But further, we worship the Risen One who asks that we die to self, that is, that we give ourselves away, in order to follow him and live in the reality of the resurrection. Expect to offer yourself whenever the Risen Christ comes near.

Fifth, *expect to depart worship a different person.* This cuts two ways. On one hand, many of us do not like change, and religion does tend to reinforce this attitude in as much as part of the basic dynamic of religion is to be a conservative force. We want this sense of being anchored, of stability, and any call to change meets with resistance. But how can we not be changed in the presence of the Light and Life of the world? I occasionally have the odd experience of climbing into a pulpit just as someone in the congregation is turning down his or her hearing aid. I hardly know whether to laugh or cry. That person seems to me to be doing everything in his or her power to avoid a thought or word that might call him or her to be a changed and transformed person.

On the other hand, we may leave resurrectional worship expecting to be altered, molded in a new way, and yet nothing seems to have happened. We leave a little disappointed and disillusioned. When that occurs we need to remember that our feelings and our perceptions are not accurate measurements of the action of the Risen Christ. It is only in hindsight that we can gauge if and when Jesus has been present. We do not use a thermometer to measure air pressure, and we should not try to use our in-the-present-moment feeling to evaluate the activity of Christ in our lives. The promise of worship is that Jesus will be there in word and sacrament, in our prayers and hymns, in our fellowship with the baptized, and that is what we need to trust more than our perceptions. Whether we are aware of it or not, the Risen One is at work.

Have you ever had lunch with a friend and got so caught up in the conversation that you were not especially aware of what or how much you ate? You leave feeling neither full nor empty, but later in the day, as you look back over the afternoon, you see that you had enough energy to do your job. The food altered you, and you did not sense it. In resurrectional worship you will leave a different person. Expect it.

Sixth, *expect to pray.* When most of us use the word "prayer," what springs to mind is making requests of God. We classify that as intercessory prayer, and it is certainly a part of any understanding of resurrectional worship. Indeed, the Prayers of People serve as a good example. But what I am suggesting is understanding the whole Liturgy of the Eucharist as prayer. At the altar rail we bring all that we have and are and give it to Christ, and Christ gives us the fullness of his presence. Given this interpretation, prayer becomes the practice of laying before Jesus the whole of our lives. We give him a tour of what is happening to us, who we are, where we are joyful and where we hurt. It is all there, spread out for him to see.

As you may sense it takes a deal of honesty and courage to do that, as well as confidence that Christ will accept us as we are. In prayer we lay ourselves open for the Risen One, and he responds. We should not anticipate hearing his voice in our heads, but we can expect that he will bless us with his presence, and guide us and provide what we need to serve him. In my prayer I sometimes become aware of a path that I had not seen, a person I need to contact and continue to pray for, and a more graceful perspective that I am wont to have.

When I was ten years old, my parents took my sister and me on a visit to Washington, DC. Part of our itinerary included a visit to the National Archives. As we entered the great, marble central room, I was aware that this was a special place. The focus of the room was the case that held the original Declaration of Independence and Constitution. I noticed that all in the room were quiet and reflective. Here before us were the documents that have shaped our country and that continue to do so on a day-by-day basis. The mood there was akin to worship. If the Declaration of Independence can evoke awe and worship, think what the resurrection should stir in us.

In worship we come face to face with the One who has changed the world, the One who opens the Kingdom of heaven to all believers, that One who gives us unconditional life and love. Before such a One, on your knees is a good place to be.

Questions to Help You Digest the Ideas of this Chapter

1. What do your calendar and checkbook say about what you value? Is what you find there a comfort or a challenge to you?

2. If you had two or three sentences to tell a friend why it is that you attend worship, what would you say?

3. A sign of maturing discipleship is developing a Rule of Prayer. That term describes what you intend to do with your prayer life. Do you have such a Rule? If not, what would your Rule of Prayer be?

chapter 10

A Lack of Confidentiality

It has happened to us all. We hear a knock at the door, we look out the window, and we see two persons with bibles and tracts in hand. If you are like me, you respond with, "Oh, no!"

As I think about this, I realize that I have this disapproving response for at least three reasons: First, I did not ask for a visit. This is the same reason we resent telemarketing calls during dinnertime. If I had wanted to talk about the Bible, I would have invited you. Second, I know that if I allow a conversation with the callers to proceed, I will be confronted with what they believe to be my inadequate faith, belief, or manner of conversion. I know that I will never measure up to the standards of these strangers. Finally, I am just plain embarrassed for these people. They don't seem to know that educated, polite people do not indulge in this sort of thing.

Because of experiences like these, the words "evangelism" and "witnessing" leave a bad taste in our mouths. For most of us, we would rather have a root canal than go door to door for Jesus. But if we have been listening to the Sunday gospel readings in church and paying attention to the resurrection stories we have been exploring, we know that we are called to *some form* of evangelism and witness. We sometimes try to release ourselves from this hook by saying that our witness will be our actions, but I suspect that many of us know deep down that is not enough. We know that actions need interpretation and that some occasions call for the clarity of words. Still, we cannot even imagine ourselves with Bible and prayer book in hand, making cold calls to strangers on Saturday morning. No, thank you. I will take a pass on this evangelism thing.

What is behind this pointed discomfort we feel about evangelism? Why is it such a tender spot in our minds? For one thing, in our society we believe that religion is a private matter. It is between God and me, and well-mannered people do not talk about religion and politics—even though they may be two of the most important things to talk about. To speak about religion feels like an invasion of privacy, even a lack of confidence about something too personal to discuss in public. Test this out at the next informal gathering you attend. I think you will find that folks are more willing to reveal their sex lives than their religious faith.

Beyond that lies another assumption: that one's religious belief cannot be challenged or questioned. It takes something as extreme as various religious groups in the Middle East—including Christians—bombing and shooting each other before we are willing to say that something has gone afoul in a belief system. Yet who of us would agree to lead a discussion group whose purpose was to decide on which one of the various groups held the highest moral and theological ground? No one!

Moreover, who am I to say that my way is better than yours? This asks for an intellectual and moral judgment that most of us do not feel qualified to make. How can I know your mind and heart so well that I can evaluate what you should believe? In our

"I'm OK–You're OK" society, I dare not make pronouncements about the adequacy or inadequacy of your beliefs. We are left with no word to offer.

So, here we are. We live in a world that says a great big NO to evangelism and witnessing, and yet we are aware that the scriptures and the tradition of the church lay before us an outgoing faith that asks us to state where we stand about the Risen Lord. This places us between the proverbial rock and hard place.

Once again the accounts of the resurrection offer us some much-needed perspectives on the touchy subject of evangelism. In the gospel according to Mark, the little group of women have gone to Jesus' tomb, found it empty, and are addressed by a young man in a white robe perched on the right side of the tomb. After telling the women that Jesus has been raised, he instructs them in an evangelical tone: "But go, tell his disciples and Peter that he is going ahead of you to Galilee; there you will see him" (Mark 16:7). Go and tell. That well might serve as a description of evangelism.

Or consider the Risen Christ's final instructions to his apostles after the resurrection in the gospel according to Luke: "You are witnesses of these things" (Luke 24:48). This expands our definition of evangelism. Go and tell, because you are witnesses of the resurrection.

Finally, in the gospel according to Matthew, we again find the apostles in Galilee after the resurrection, and there Christ is giving his farewell speech: "Go therefore and make disciples of all nations, baptizing them in the name of the Father and of the Son and of the Holy Spirit, and teaching them to obey everything that I have commanded you" (Matt. 28:19–20). This fills out our definition a bit more. Again, the word is to go, a reminder that our religion has always been a missionary one. The going and telling based on what we have witnessed is to include teaching, a call to obedience to all of Jesus' teaching and to baptism.

These resurrection stories, then, give us a simple, succinct, and workable understanding of our call from the Risen Lord to be evangelists and witnesses. We may not like it, but there it is, straightforward and simple.

It would be hard to understand The Episcopal Church today without reference to *The Book of Common Prayer's* liturgy for Holy Baptism. Included in that liturgy is The Baptismal Covenant. In baptism, the God of the resurrection acts on us and joins us to Christ's death and resurrection. Part of the liturgy makes this clear. "In [the waters of baptism] we are buried with Christ in his death. By it we share in his resurrection" (p. 306)" But the covenant also states our response to God's gracious action in baptism. The covenant takes the form of questions and answers. The first three deal with belief as encapsulated in the three articles of the Apostles' Creed. Then follow five questions about behavior. Question three is straightforward: "Will you proclaim by word and example the Good News of God in Christ?" And the people reply: "I will, with God's help" (pp. 304–305). The Baptismal Covenant puts us squarely before Jesus, who tells us to go, tell, and witness.

If we return to Luke's gospel, we will find some material that will help us refine our definition some more. The word "witness" in that crucially important phrase, "You are my witnesses," helps nuance our developing definition even more. The sense of it is conveyed as someone giving testimony in a court. It is to attest to what one knows on the basis of first-hand experience and observation.

In the previous verse (Luke 24:47) and running parallel to witness is the word "proclaim." This has a public quality to it, in the sense that it suggests making an announcement, sometimes an announcement of great importance.

From this exercise in etymology, we can conclude that our going, telling, and witnessing is grounded in personal experience. Further, by that experience we have the conviction that what we proclaim is of great importance and that our telling has an open, public quality.

We should also carefully note what this biblical material does not say. There is no sense that I, at least, can perceive that our witness is to have a coercive or strong-arm quality to it. As I was driving recently, I had the rare opportunity to see a badger beside the road. They are reclusive animals and seldom observed. They keep to themselves, but if they ever get their teeth into something, they never let go. That is not a model for evangelism: either hiding our commitment to Christ or never letting go of a person, besieging them, or just plain bothering them.

Further, I can find no promise that we will always succeed in our evangelism efforts as persons or as the church. To put it another way, our witness may be rejected. As we point to the Risen One, the response may be, "No, thank you." I can name some churches that have given an evangelism program a shot, but it did not reap great and instant results, so they gave up. We should know from the outset that not everyone wants to know and follow the Risen Lord.

Finally, I can find no hint that we should take the blame if evangelism is not successful. That is, the results are not in our hands. One of the most liberating things I ever heard about evangelism is this: there really is only one evangelist, and that is the Holy Spirit. All we do is speak a word, plant a seed, state our experience. And then we let it go. Success is not our goal.

Let's pull all of this together. We can state that the Risen Lord tells us to go, witness, and tell others about him, to base what we say on our own experience and observations, to proceed with a sense that what we are saying is vitally important, to go public, and to leave the rest to him. We do not see confrontation, badgering, shaming, or threatening as part of our portfolio. We have no need to proclaim in such a way as to embarrass others or ourselves. And all of this is based on what we ourselves know, that Jesus is Victor; we do not need to be biblical scholars or theological experts to do this. In short, we tell what we know and whom we love. That's it!

If we take away Jesus as the subject of this definition, we can find many examples of our witnessing on the basis of personal experience. It is something we do all the time. For instance, my daughters keep me informed about what movies they have seen and which ones they think are good enough for me to see. The text message often reads, "You will love it." Since I know and trust them, my interest in their recommendations grows, and sometimes I even see the movie.

I am a member of a local wine club. At least once a month I go to the store, walk to the temperature-controlled cellar, proceed to my bin, and pick up the wines that the wine merchant has selected. I usually set aside some time when I go to his store, because I want to know about wine, and I know that he has an astonishingly deep knowledge of this rather complex subject. For him, this is a labor of love, and he relishes talking about the production and unique qualities of each of the wines in his store. I recently asked for a certain style of wine, and he showed me three choices out of the several dozen possibilities in the store. We chatted about their qualities, and finally he put his finger on one and said, "You will love this one." And I did. This is witnessing. It is evangelism, with wine as the subject. It is based on experience and observations, and a sense that sharing this is a wonderful thing to do. "I really enjoy talking to people about wine," he says and it shows.

What might this look like in a church? I think we can identify three considerations that would promote the sort of evangelism we have been looking at in a local church. First, we must be clear that our church is a place where people can find and be found by Christ. I cannot think of any other reason why a person would want to be part of a congregation apart from that. If we understand our church as a comfortable family or a place that "meets my needs," we have wandered away from the point, which is to meet Jesus. My own observation is that we—and I include myself—get carried away by all sorts of distractions in our working in and planning for the church. And some of these are even good things, if we can keep them in their proper, subsidiary place. One of the churches in the Diocese of Montana has a motto that is displayed prominently on the signs outside the church. It is only three words: "We celebrate Christ." That's exactly as it should be.

Second, we should be able to identify the ways and means that we have been blessed and transformed by our encounters with the Risen One in our congregations. One of the questions I often ask vestries as part of my official visitations is: What resurrectional and transformational things are happening among you? Sometimes there is a bit of hesitancy, but once they begin to talk, often example after example spill out.

The cathedral of this diocese has recently gone through the transition of the retirement of a dean and rector, and the discernment process for a new dean and rector. During that time I have been fascinated by what members value in the cathedral parish. A transition seems to help people surface to their consciousness the good things in their church. We heard: we value the social outreach of this church, we like the Christian formation program, we look forward to fine preaching and liturgy, and we appreciate the openness of the congregation to all sorts of people. These are signs of the presence of the Risen Lord. These are testimonies of resurrection and transformation. People, left to themselves, do not usually worry about the poor and about rearing children in the faith; rather, care for the poor and children are signs of the presence of the Risen One.

Third, evangelism in the church begins with its members speaking a good word about the church in the larger community. In one way or another, all of us are presented with occasions when we can say that the church is a place of blessing, that our church does exciting things, that the priest is a model of a faithful pastor, that we are accepted as a part of an intimate community. Those statements are the opening gambit, and some will want to pursue that conversation. Behind all the examples above stands the Risen Lord, because these examples are instances of his presence and activity. So there will be occasions that allow us in a natural way to name the name of Jesus the Risen Christ.

We have been thinking together about positive ways that churches can do evangelism. But there are factors that amount to shooting ourselves in the foot. Speaking a bad word in public about the church does great damage. We all know that negative news travels faster than positive news, and that is doubly true when a church member denigrates his own congregation. Church fights will kill any energy for evangelism quicker than almost anything else. Gossip, clannishness, and negative reviews of the priest and bishop do not help in any way. I was recently talking with a person who had visited a local congregation. She said, "As soon as you stepped through the door, you could feel the toxicity. I would never go there."

So, that's congregational evangelism. But as much as some might want to hear it, the evangelism of churches is based on personal evangelism. A church can prepare itself to welcome people; it can advertise and it can have the best priest in the world, but someone somewhere has to testify to the resurrection at work in that church community. It boils down to you and me. At the outset of the chapter, we noted some of the reasons we do not like to get involved in evangelism and witnessing. That, however, asks us to ponder whether there is a way to do evangelism that is the genuine thing, that fits the biblical definition we developed, and that allows us to testify in a natural and non-confrontive way. That's what we need to work on.

First, we need to begin with the awareness that the Lord is present and active in our world and lives, and we have to be able to tell how that has worked in our lives. Years ago I attended a workshop on congregational and personal evangelism. One of our exercises was to choose a partner and go to a quiet place to talk. Our assignment was to tell each other our God story—those times when, those places where, and those persons in whom we sense the presence and guidance of the Lord. We could use a timeline approach, we were told, or we could just jump in with the first episode that came to mind. I thought to myself, "This will take about two and a half minutes." I believed that I had little to say. So, I found a partner and we set to work. I began. One incident of Christ's presence reminded me of another, and on it went. After four and a half hours, I was still talking, but dinnertime had arrived. We all need to spend some serious time with this or a similar exercise. Some make spiritual timelines on long sheets of paper.

I have a friend who did this and worked on it for months. The last time I checked the timeline, it was twelve feet long. Others work well with journaling. And some of us like conversation best.

Allow me to use The Episcopal Church again as an example. It is a little known but true fact that part of the canon law of this church requires that all members be trained in knowing and sharing their God stories. It's a canon frequently forgotten.

Knowing our God stories constitutes the first step. The next step is sharing it. At first this rattles us a bit. This is just what we think we want to avoid. But think of it in this alternative way:

- All of us from time to time have serious conversations with others. Often this occurs with a friend or family member, but sometimes it happens with a stranger.

- These conversations sometimes consist of heavy doses of personal sharing. It could begin with a chat about a book, a work problem, a recent trip, or an almost infinite number of other topics.

- The sharing may well take the form of "My experience has been . . ." or "I believe that. . . ."

- Next, there is absolutely nothing socially or personally wrong with sharing an experience that involves the Risen Christ. We usually keep this sort of thing in confidence, but this is one place where a lack of confidentiality is recommended. Suppose the other person confides that she is going through a period where she seems to have lost her way and is no longer certain why she gets out of bed in the morning. Christians have something to say about that! The resurrection addresses that issue! Why would we keep quiet about the sense of purpose and joy in our lives that is a part of living the resurrection? I can imagine the response to the woman being, "I know what you mean. I have times like that. But I have discovered that the closer I walk with Christ, the less these things seem to bother me." That's it. Two sentences. You have planted the seed. You have stated what you know to be true. The other person may choose to pursue it or may simply turn the conversation in a new direction. In either case, it is OK. Here's another possible answer, "I know what you mean. I have times like that. But what happens to me in my church community helps me a lot." You have done all you need to do. That is personal evangelism.

- Finally, there are occasions when we need gently to offer an occasion for action or commitment. We might say, "Can I pick you up next Sunday and introduce you to my church?" And sometimes the other person opens the door. For instance, I have a doctor friend who works mostly with terminal patients. She tells me that for reasons she cannot identify, patients ask her to pray with them. She says this always takes her aback, but that she does in fact pray with the patient. Witnessing can involve an invitation to action.

More than a quarter of a century ago, I received a phone call from my brother-in-law telling me that my father had died. It was sudden and unexpected. He had simply passed away in his sleep at the age of fifty-eight. I packed up my family and made a quick trip home. When I pulled into the driveway of my parents' house, my mother was waiting for me. The moment I had dreaded was about to arrive. I had no idea what state she was in or what she might need from me. She hugged me, and as she did so, she said, "I don't know how people can get through this without God." This was her witness and testimony. I suspect I was not the only person she shared that comment with. She said exactly what I needed at that horrible time.

Go. Tell. Witness.

Questions to Help You Tackle the Tough Subject of Evangelism

1. When someone talks about their faith with you, how do you feel? Why?
2. What resurrectional things are happening in your church?
3. How is the Risen Lord ministering to you at this time in your life?
4. Would you feel able to share your answer to question 3 with someone else?

chapter 11

Earth Care

When people hear that I am from Montana, they often reply simply by repeating the state's unofficial nickname, "Big Sky Country." That is an apt description for the state. Especially in the eastern part of Montana, the sky seems to extend forever and is colored that azure blue characteristic of high elevations. No one has been able to explain to me why it appears so large, but I can state that it is bigger than anywhere else I have been. Under the sky are vast high prairies, golden brown in color, and badlands that seem cut out of the rock by giants.

In the western part of the state are what I am told are the most rugged parts of the Rocky Mountains. Much of the year they are snow capped and catch clouds in their peaks. The mountain ranges are separated by alpine valleys often filled with deer, elk, and bison. Rivers cut through the mountains, including the mighty Missouri. When I invite people to visit Montana, I tell them I will show them where God lives. I say that because it hints at the awesome majesty and stunning beauty of the place.

After I moved to Montana and spent some time here, I came to realize that for all its massive mountains and vast prairies, it is an extraordinarily fragile place. The awe the landscape inspires tends to inure people to how easily it can be marred and ruined.

Because it is a dry area, water has to be handled carefully and water tables constantly monitored. Montana is rich in timber and minerals, but extracting those has sometimes blighted the earth. It is strong and weak at the same time. People need to tread carefully in such a setting.

More and more we are learning—sometimes the hard way—that we must give the earth tender, loving care. Our history of that caregiving has been poor. If the best predictor of future behavior is past behavior, the earth itself faces scary and dangerous prospects.

Christians have some culpability in the misuse of these God-given natural resources. Part of this lack of concern has to be an overemphasis on the soul and spirit. I have a suspicion that many of our friends and families who choose not to associate themselves with the church have the impression that our primary focus is the psyche and the inner life. To the degree that that has been true, we have ignored our bodies, our society, and the earth itself. Sometimes we have not been able to adopt a holistic view of life as followers of Jesus. We have, I believe, too narrowly focused on a certain aspect of ourselves.

The scriptures themselves have not always helped us understand our responsibility for the earth. Perhaps the chief culprit is one of the most well-known and popular parts of the Bible. I speak of the story of creation. This material has been so misused that we need to spend some time with it in order to understand how we have gone awry.

First, a careful reading of the first three chapters of Genesis reveals that there are two creation stories, not one. The first portrays God speaking the world into existence in seven days (Genesis 1:1–2:3). The second has the flavor of a folk tale, with God creating the first human out of mud and placing that being in a life-giving garden (Gen. 2:4–3:23). In our thinking about our responsibility for the earth, it will be helpful to keep in mind the distinctive natures of the two accounts.

The majestic first creation story narrates God's activity in terms of seven days. On the sixth day God creates a male and a female and places them in a world now replete with sun and moon, plants and animals. Then God puts humanity in a supervisory position in regard to the world.

> The God said, "Let us make humankind in our image, according to our likeness; and let them have dominion over the fish of the sea, and over the birds of the air, and over the cattle, and over all the wild animals of the earth, and over every creeping thing that creeps upon the earth" . . . God blessed [the man and woman], and God said to them, "Be fruitful and multiply, and fill the earth and subdue it; and have dominion over the fish of the sea and over the birds of the air and over every living thing that moves on the earth." God said, "See, I have given you every plant yielding seed that is upon the face of all the earth, and every tree with seed in its fruit; you shall have them for food." (Gen. 1:26, 28–29)

Over the centuries the words "dominion" and "subdue" appear to have been the terms we hear most clearly in this account. Given an almost God-like nature and position, humanity is charged with running the zoo. The same is implied but not overtly stated in regard to the flora of the earth; God seems to say, "The plants are there for you, so use them." These are commands of God that we have readily obeyed, but we have not done it well. We cut down the rain forests and drove species into extinction. We choke ourselves on our own pollution and ravage the earth in search of its resources.

This is no Garden of Eden in which we now live.

We can, however, take a different slant on this text, and that will make a great distinction. What might it imply if we understood that our God-like image and capabilities were to be used in a God-like way?

What if we could hear God saying that we are to "subdue" and "dominate" in the manner in which God would do that? The world is God's creation, lovingly brought into being and delightful to God. We might say that the world is God's child, and that God wants us to treat it with that in mind. What if we were to understand the terms in the sense of ordering and protecting as a rancher takes care of his cattle and land? That different slant changes everything, does it not?

The second creation story beginning at Genesis 2:4 starts with a barren and dry earth. God first creates man out of the dust of the ground, and then proceeds to plant a pleasant and pleasing garden in which the man may dwell. Later God creates the animals so that the man would not need to be alone, and the man is given the privilege of naming them, suggesting a certain power over the fauna presented to him. None of the animals are able to serve as an adequate partner for the man, so God creates woman.

To make a backward step, at the point where God has created the garden, he takes the man and puts him in the garden. The man is commanded to "till it and keep it" (Gen. 2:15). Again there are implications that humanity can "use" the earth and its creatures. The dangerous word in the story may be the order to "keep" the earth, which to our ears suggests ownership and authority. In the original language, however, the word keep can easily and properly be translated as "serve." For me, at least, that is an extraordinarily powerful idea, to serve the earth. This suggests tender care of and delighting in the planet. In this second story, it is a gift from God to man to sustain him both physically and emotionally. The accounts say our responsibility is to treat it for what it is, a precious gift.

A careful and nuanced reading of the creation stories begins to pull us back from our sense that we can do to the earth and its creatures whatever is profitable and pleasing to us, that we can use the earth for our own ends minus any sense of care and service. If we next introduce the category of resurrection, we are led to even deeper and richer veins in our thinking. We can proceed in several steps as we explore this approach.

First, the "what" that God raised was a body. That seems so obvious that at first glance we may think we hardly need to mention it. We need to pause and think about that as our first stage. The means by which the victory of God's life and love is manifested to the whole cosmos is a physical thing, a genuine human body. In the language of the book of Genesis, the body is shaped from the dust of the earth, dust we can hold in our hands and blow away with our breath. The pivot point in history takes place through the agency of Jesus' body. Notice that God did not use an idea or a bit of wisdom or a teaching to accomplish God's plan of reconciliation. It was the physical, the human, the touchable and visible body that God chose. We should, therefore, not take the physicality of the resurrection lightly.

Second, the resurrected Lord appeared in a transformed and glorified body. We have already dealt with this in our study of 1 Corinthians 15. No ghost, no apparition, no mental projection was the Risen One. He was physically present, but now in a body that had been transformed so that it was beyond decay, disease, and death. This presses the boundaries of our thinking beyond our usual assumptions, but that may well be part of the point. Here it is this: the physical remains physical, genuine and touchable, but now made new. The crucified body of Jesus is the risen body of Jesus, transformed and glorified.

As a side note, notice that the New Testament almost always speaks of the Christian hope for the future in terms of this resurrection body, not in terms of the immortality of the soul. Life in the age to come is a gift from God in that who we are remains who we are, but made new so that we are beyond the cold hand of death. Further, the Nicene Creed says that our belief in "life everlasting" takes the form of the "resurrection of the body." So both scripture and tradition have spoken clearly on this matter.

With step three we move into new territory. Our scriptural guide is Paul as he writes in the eighth chapter of his letter to the Romans. A word of warning is appropriate. The letter to the Romans is a work of transcendental majesty and complexity; it is a closely and carefully argued document. We will need to proceed with caution and attention.

Chapter eight opens with one of Paul's many uses of "therefore." He inserts that word to alert us that he has concluded one movement in his thinking and is now proceeding to a new movement of thought. Verse one reads: "There is therefore now no condemnation for those who are in Christ Jesus" (Rom. 8:1).

In the first seven chapters, he has shown that all humanity without exception stands before God as rebellious people worthy of condemnation. Then he proceeds to show that God's primary motive is not to condemn, but rather God, in an act of divine grace, has chosen to set right God's relationship with humanity, an act accomplished through the unique agency of the death and resurrection of Jesus Christ.

Thus we arrive at the first verse of chapter eight. What Paul is proclaiming is that in Christ we see a paradigm shift in God's dealings with humankind. "For the law of the Spirit of life in Christ Jesus has set you free from the law of sin and of death" (Rom. 8:2).

What follows in chapter eight is a lively and honest discussion about the struggle we feel between the part of us that wants to live on our own terms apart from God and the part of us transformed by resurrection. In crass terms, it's the struggle between the little devil on one shoulder and the good angel on the other. Then Paul mentions something that we know from other sources has been a part of his life as an itinerant apostle, namely, suffering.

With the mention of suffering, Paul moves to a set of ideas that will be very helpful to us.

> I consider that the sufferings of this present time are not worth comparing with the glory about to be revealed to us. For the creation waits with eager longing for the revealing of the children of God; for the creation was subjected to futility, not of its own will but by the will of the one who subjected it, in hope that the creation itself will be set free from its bondage to decay and will obtain the freedom of the glory of the children of God. We know that the whole creation has been groaning in labor pains until now; and not only the creation, but we ourselves, who have the first fruits of the Spirit, groan inwardly while we wait for adoption, the redemption of our bodies. (Rom. 8:18–23)

The riches of this text are almost more than the mind can take in, but we can, nevertheless, note several points. To start, notice that in the future, full redemption toward which Christians look will take the form of transformation and resurrection of our bodies. We have often mentioned that the shape of the Christian life and the pattern that identifies the action of God is the Paschal Mystery, the dying and rising of Christ. Paul extends that paradigm to its limit and end point: the resurrection of our bodies will be like the resurrection of Christ. The Risen Lord, then, is our future. We will be like him.

St. Paul also introduces an unexpected and stunning idea: the whole creation groans in anticipation of this resurrectional future. Our own sense that we are on a journey to something better, with the best yet to come, is shared by creation itself. The Paschal Mystery, our participation in it via baptism, and the future of the cosmos are all tied together in the plan of God. The resurrected and transformed body of Christ, our resurrection and transformation, and the renewal of the whole word are all of a piece.

We, then, are harbingers of the future, in as much as the gifts of the Spirit demonstrate that we are truly part of God's coming new creation. In various letters, Paul gives attention to the gifts of the Spirit, which he sees as signs that we belong to the Risen One. For Paul the Spirit is the Lord, as he puts it. So, the ability to believe and say that Jesus is Lord, and the attitude of hope in a resurrected future, are gifts of the Spirit. And that makes us living examples of God at work, shaping a transformed and renewed world.

We have explored the accounts of creation in Genesis, reminded ourselves of the physicality of the resurrection body, and have looked at Paul's linking of our resurrectional future and that of the whole world. From this, we uncover three simple but important implications.

- God's work of resurrection, renewal, and transformation is not focused simply and only on us. God's plan involves the whole of God's creation. Twenty years ago or so my wife and I were in London on vacation, and we visited St. James' Church,

Piccadilly, on Sunday. It is an ancient congregation housed in a classic Christopher Wren building. Near the pulpit was a large painting of the church just as it appeared when you walked in from the busy street. During the presentation of the offering and the preparation of the altar for Communion, two acolytes went to the painting and opened it. I had not noticed that it was a triptych and that we had been looking at it in its closed form. The acolytes opened it to reveal a new scene. In the center was the St. James' Wren building, but around it was a colorful and detailed view of the city and the countryside, changed and renewed. It was a picture of heaven, of course: the world we know now, church and cosmos, transformed in the beautiful reality that is God's plans for all of creation. I found this extraordinarily powerful, in as much as we were about to participate in receiving the transformed bread and wine in the sacrament that is the foretaste of things to come. It's not just about us; it's about everything.

- We are agents of the resurrection. As baptized persons we are authorized to act on behalf of the Risen Lord and to carry on his work. Our work is proclaiming the gospel, nurturing people in the faith, caring for the poor, and working for justice and peace. But we need to add one more thing: we are also to care for the earth itself, which is loved by God and is part of God's plan of salvation. As a child I loved to play cowboy. Besides the cap pistol and the imaginary horse, an essential part of the outfit was my sheriff's badge. That was the sign that I was on the side of justice and peace. Our baptism is our badge, our sign that we are authorized agents of resurrection.

- While we have our work to do, we know that only God can fully transform the world. Only God can empower resurrection. We have a vocation as God's agents, and we are to give our best to that, but we can also relax in the knowledge that at the end only God can bring about the fullness of the new creation. And God will do just that.

Between 1984 and 1990 the Anglican Communion worked on a proclamation called "The Five Marks of Mission." I am told that when they were first discussed, they provoked controversy. In 1996 they were officially adopted by the Communion, and in 2009 The Episcopal Church officially approved them. The first two are no surprise: to preach Good News of the Kingdom, and to teach, baptize, and nurture new believers. The next two are likely the cause of some of the controversy: to respond to human need by loving service, and to seek to transform unjust structures of society. The last remains, I believe, the mark that we have done the least to implement: to strive to safeguard the integrity of creation, and to sustain and renew the life of the earth. We are beginning to understand just how integral the care of the earth is to the mission of God in the world.

My prayer is that this walk through the scriptures has made an airtight case for the necessity of Christian people to be in the forefront of protecting, nurturing, and caring for the earth itself. Our record has not always been good, but we now have a chance to set that right. Further, I pray that this study has served to empower and energize us for working on this fifth mark of mission.

What might it look like if we were to pursue this part of our baptismal ministry? What might we need to do?

First, we will need to alter our mindset. For many, the care of creation is not on their intellectual horizon. A place to begin would be to remind ourselves over and over that what God wants for us is what God wants for the creation. Our future is resurrection, and so is creation's.

My father promised me that if I graduated from college, he would get me a car. True to his word, upon graduation he presented me with a wonderful 1963 Dodge with a huge engine. He had purchased it at a good price, because it needed some repair, which he did himself. I had not taken his promise entirely seriously, so that car was a surprise. I loved that car, which I have to admit was capable of running at 120 mph. It got me where I needed to go and I was proud to be seen in it. Because it was a loving gift that delighted me, I took good care of that car, I babied it, and I took care of it to the limits of my mechanical knowledge and available tools. What might happen to our mindset if we could see the earth in the way I saw that car?

Second, we can become models of how to care for the earth. As you look around, how many of your friends appear to be involved in any serious effort whatsoever to nurture the world? My guess is not many. Several of the congregations in the Diocese of Montana have developed community gardens on land that was not being used. They till and serve the land, and they use the fruits of the earth to serve by giving the produce to food banks. You can't go by those churches without seeing the gardens. It's a sign of mission and a model of care of the world. We need more gardens and other models to inspire us.

Third, we can advocate for the earth. We can be evangelists for the world. Earlier we noted that Christians need to serve the Risen One in both word and deed. So, too, word and deed are required in our service to the world. What form might that take for you in your neck of the woods?

I live in Helena, the capital of Montana, a city nestled a mile up in the heart of the Rockies. Overlooking the city is Mt. Helena, a city park and a source of pride and pleasure. From the summit is a breathtaking view of the city, the Helena valley, and the Big Belt and Cascade mountain ranges. One day my dog and I were hiking up the mountain and we came across a cairn, a carefully constructed pile of stones. There were not signs or posters explaining it, but there it silently stood. I immediately thought of the stories in Hebrew scriptures when people erected cairns to mark important events, such as the spot where God had wrestled with Jacob or the place where the Israelites first crossed the Jordon River into the promised land. My dog and I simply stood and looked at the stones. What significance did it mark? For me it marked a pleasant summer day with my dog. It marked the care of the city for its largest park. It marked an awareness of the physicality of the world. Beauty and wonder were as present and real as a pile of rocks. The creation of God is as touchable as a stone. God's delight in the beauty and variety of the world was as close as a cairn. Earth care. We can do that!

Questions to Help Fill Out the Shape of Our Mission to the World

1. Can you make a list of our misuse of both the fauna and flora of the world? What one item concerns you the most?

2. What items would you put on a list of the concrete actions individuals and families can do to serve the earth?

3. What items would you put on a list of concrete actions churches can do to serve the earth?

4. What do you see as the biggest obstacle to this mark of mission? What can be done to address it?

chapter 12

And We End in a Garden

Both the scriptural story and this book began in a garden, which serves as a symbol for life as God intends it to be. As you think back to the second chapter of Genesis, remember that in this wonderful place there exists an abundance of everything needed for life and peace. The trees and plants produce abundant fruit, the man and the woman live in harmony with each other and with all other living things in Eden. Contentment, a balance of work and rest, calm—these describe the life of the man and the woman. All of these qualities are epitomized in the intimate relationship of God with the man, the woman, and the garden.

This was Eden, even for us today a word that evokes life at its best. But even as we say the word, we know that there is no Eden in this life. We know that we live in a world of jarring disharmony; we certainly cannot describe our lives as balanced and peaceful. Something has gone terribly wrong.

Now we fast-forward to the conclusion of the story of the scriptures. We pick up the narrative in the Revelation to John, and we quickly realize that we end the journey in a garden.

Then the angel showed me the river of the water of life, bright as crystal, flowing from the throne of God and of the Lamb through the middle of the street of the city. On either side of the river is the tree of life with its twelve kinds of fruit, producing its fruit each month; and the leaves of the tree are for the healing of the nations. Nothing accursed will be found there any more. But the throne of God and of the Lamb will be in it, and his servants will worship him; they will see his face, and his name will be on their foreheads. And there will be no more night; they need no light of lamp or sun, for the Lord God will be their light, and they will reign forever and ever. (Rev. 22:1–5)

We need to study this passage with the proper frame of reference. There are many books that attempt to deal with the book of Revelation as if it provided a map of the future if one had the right key to unlock the book's imagery. We would miss the depth and richness of this astonishing book if we took that approach.

Revelation was written by a man named John who had been sentenced to a penal colony on the island of Patmos in the Mediterranean Sea. His crime, he tells us, was that he had been preaching about Jesus, the Risen One. John writes the book, actually a long letter, to seven churches in what today we know as Turkey. These congregations are under the pressure of ostracism and persecution from the local authorities, and, indeed, there had already been one member martyred. The churches could realistically expect things only to get worse. The letter-book presents itself as a vision from God given to John one Sunday. Revelation is a beautifully written, complex work, rich with images and ideas from the Hebrew scriptures, and portrays both events in heaven and God's plan for these persecuted churches in Turkey. The overarching point of the revelation to John is rooted in the resurrection of Jesus Christ: God will be acting according to the pattern of the

Paschal Mystery with respect to the seven churches, but also with respect to the entire cosmos and the entire span of history. God will be victorious over all, will bring life out of death, will guide and guard the church, and will restore the entire universe to harmony and peace.

The chief actors in John's vision are the One who sits on the throne, a circumlocution for God, and the Lamb who sits by the throne. As the vision unfolds we are told the Lamb had been killed but now lives. We are led through a series of visions based on the perfect number seven, and in every situation it is the Lamb alone, once dead and now alive, that is capable of revealing and carrying out God's salvific plan for the church and the world.

With this background we can turn again to the closing vision of Revelation recorded above. Here is a list of the elements in this climatic episode:

- God and the Lamb, working in perfect unanimity, reign forever and ever.

- Crystal clear, pure water flows from the God and the Lamb.

- On the banks of the urban garden in the transformed city of new Jerusalem grows the tree of life, the same tree we first encountered in the story of the first Eden.

- The tree produces fruit every month.

- The fruit of the tree of life brings healing to all peoples.

- The faithful servants of God and the Lamb will worship God and the Lamb, will see God face to face, and will forever carry the name of God on their foreheads. Part of the wonder of this detail in the vision is that in the Old Testament tradition, no one could see God and survive the experience. Moreover, the name of God on the foreheads of the servants recalls the marking of the cross on the forehead of a newly baptized person.

- Nothing accursed, nothing that disrupts the reconciliation of God and the whole created order, will be in the garden of the new Jerusalem.

- The radiance of God alone provides light, that is, nothing evil breaks through the divine glory.

- And the servants of God will reign with God and the Lamb forever.

I find this a breathtaking vision of the future of God's people, the church. Surely the persecuted Christians to and for whom John writes were also "blown away." This revelation of the future of the church instills hope, courage, and perseverance in the face of sometimes hostile forces. Throughout the last two millennia, Christians have endured many occasions that sucked the hope out of them. But here in this vision we find the antidote, able to restore courage and renewed commitment.

So, all creation will be restored and we will be back in Eden. We will know God fully, walk with God, receive God's blessing forever. This is the vision of the future that transforms us. This is the vision that empowers us to continue in the mission of God despite setbacks, failure, and antagonism.

I love mystery novels, and I am nearly always reading one. As I write this, for example, I am working my way through the Sherlock Holmes stories and enjoying every minute of it. In some mysteries the tension about how the case will be solved is too great, and I flip to the back of the book and see how it all ends. But most of the time I do not succumb to that temptation, because it is the nature of mystery novels that order will overcome chaos and that justice will be served. I believe that is part of the unconscious appeal of this sort of literature; it affirms that life is not, at root, tragic.

This concluding vision from the pen of John works in a similar way for the church. We may not know what twists and turns lie ahead in the journey of life, but we do know that the end of our story, as individuals and as church, will be God's victory of life and love, a victory that includes us.

The door of the empty Easter tomb is the entrance into this transformed future, in this new reality. Our calling is to step out of the dark, cold tomb and into the eternal light of the Risen Lord, the Lamb who was slain but now lives. Our problem is that while life in the old reality is dark and cold, it is, at least, familiar to us. We live. We die. End of story. That describes the shape of life in the tomb. The Risen One turns around, as he did with Mary Magdalene in the account of Easter morning found in John's gospel and speaks our name. (For the sake of clarity, the writer of John's gospel is not the same person who wrote Revelation; then, as now, John was a common name.) This is the invitation to walk into the new, unfamiliar, sometimes scary, but always adventure-filled Easter reality. One of the letters in the New Testament says it better than I: "Beloved, we are God's children now; what we will be has not yet been revealed. What we do know is this: when he is revealed, we will be like him, for we will see him as he is" (1 John 3:2). To put it simply, our future is Jesus Christ the Risen Lord.

When I travel I often carry with me in my briefcase a small icon. I have several that I put to this use, but the most frequent traveling companion is called, Christ the Judge of All. I place the icon in front of me at meetings and on the desk in the hotel room. If we can understand icons as windows into heaven, they can be extraordinarily useful in prayer and in calling us to center ourselves in Christ. This particular icon, Christ the Pantocrator or Christ the Judge of All, shows the Lord from the waist up looking directly at the viewer. He is dressed in the violet, blue, and gold clothing of a king. In his left hand he holds a closed book. Around his head is a halo with "I am" written in Greek letters; that phrase, "I am," is how God identifies himself to Moses in the burning bush story in Exodus. The background is gold, representing heavenly glory and light. And Christ's right hand is lifted in the gesture of blessing.

I carry this image when I am on a journey. In it I see heavenly glory, the glory of God and the Lamb that will be fully revealed at the end of the ages, leaking out on the desk or table in front of me. And Jesus is always and forever granting blessing, grace, and mercy to all who look to him. This small icon that I tuck away in my briefcase sums up the message of this vision from John's revelation, and it does so in a single glance. It says simply: this is our hope, and this is our future—Jesus Christ, the Lamb who died but now lives.

I hope you sense this vision crafts a new view of reality and the future in us. And I find it a breathtaking and compelling power in my life. Now, three implications flow from this view of the Risen One as our hope and, indeed, as our future.

First, the vision calls us to allow a holy longing to develop in our lives and in our churches. For example, I grew up in an area and a time when truck farming was commonplace. This was a river valley where the soil was made rich by centuries of flooding and where the summer sun was intense. Along the main roads the local farmers had erected wooden huts and sheds, and during the summer they sold their goods from these. My culinary world, then, was shaped by freshly picked tomatoes, corn, green beans, and cabbage, all of which were cooked and eaten within hours of being harvested. When I left home I soon discovered that produce from other sources could barely carry a torch next to what I had known. When I buy these items today in the grocery store, I know they will not live up to my memories. The tomatoes will have a pale flavor, and the corn will simply not be sweet. I stand there in the clean, bright aisles of the store, longing for something better.

The vision of the blessed garden in the new Jerusalem calls forth that same sort of longing. We know that there is something better, more lively, more satisfying, and that we can share in it.

Part of what makes this so important is that our longings defines who we are and how we mold our lives. Consider the difference it makes in a person's life if what they desire is to watch movies on television as opposed to someone who wants to play the piano well. Think of the power of the vision of the garden. It calls forth in us a desire to be with Jesus, to be like Jesus, and to share in his mission and in his life of perfect love and community with the Father and the Spirit. That is holy longing.

Second, from the holy longing will grow the ability to change. After we settle into adulthood, most of us have arranged our lives in a way that is comfortable and convenient for us. And we do not appreciate someone who wants to alter that. Indeed, the person who rocks our boat usually earns our resentment and anger. To ourselves we may whisper, "Who does she think she is telling me how to live? Why doesn't he mind his own business and let me mind my own?"

The issue for Christians and for the church lies in our Risen Lord's call to continual conversion and transformation. When we are honest, we sense that our lives may be comfortable and convenient for us, but that we would not want Jesus to look too closely at who we are and how we live. The image we have used is that we are always being called to step out of the tomb and into the new reality of the resurrection. One of the important but over-looked style conventions in the writings of Paul is that he usually says that we are being saved, not that we are saved; it is a process that is not yet finished, and we still need to be in that process of living more and more fully into the resurrection. In short, we have to learn to live with change.

When I was in seminary, I had been assigned to work in a local church as part of a class in Christian formation. I attended worship and I assisted in a high school Sunday School class. Part of this field work experience was to write reports on my work for the professor. At the end of the course I had a meeting with the professor. I still remember him looking over my reports and saying to me, "You clearly have a tendency to too easily accept things as they are." He knew then, as I know now, that an integral part of the work of priesthood and of being a church and a disciple is to experience that holy longing and its concomitant need to change, to be transformed, to step fully into the process of being saved.

This should not be taken to mean that change for change's sake is proper. Moreover, all of us can think of changes in ourselves or our churches that have not proved to be good or helpful. And while we assert that we need to be able to change, that we have a certain flexibility of heart and mind, we also must affirm our need to be true to who we are and to assert our basic identity in Christ. I am dubious about the claims of some Christians that they know just what needs to be altered and just how to do it, usually for-warded by assertions about the virtues of creativity and innova-tion. It seems to me that these attitudes simply produce a church that lurches from one new theology, one new program, one new church growth method to another. I do not believe that innovation per se will lead us into all truth.

But the Risen Christ has promised to lead us into all truth (John 16:13). Note the two key elements: Christ, and leading into truth. The first change we need to be ready for is that initiated by the Risen One, and the second change is to be able to perceive a facet of God's truth and respond appropriately. The media for this are serious study of the scripture, deep prayer, careful listening to our own hearts and minds, and a meticulous listening to the discussions of the church. Note that these methods are as old as the church, but often produce something both profound and exciting. This approach, however, requires discernment, focus, openness to new perspectives and time.

A friend recently told me about an AA meeting he had attended. He had suggested that they spend their time together sharing reasons for being grateful. At that proposal a general groan erupted from the gathering: not another gratitude meeting. This led my friend into some profound thoughts. First, to be grateful means that we will have to stop turning in on ourselves and begin to direct ourselves in an outward direction. And, furthermore, to be grateful means that we will have to give up our delusion that we can control our lives, but instead begin to see that all the ingredients of life are gifts. It is grace, not our self-will, that defines life. When he passed on these thoughts, they had the ring of truth for me. It is little wonder, then, that gratitude and generosity are so hard to develop. In order to become grateful and generous people, the changes we need to make are to cut off our incessant self-interest and our strong need to control, and to leave ourselves open to the graces and gifts of God. The fact that the Risen Lord will lead his people into all truth liberates us to live flexible, changing lives, even while remaining true to our identity.

The third implication of this resurrectional vision of God's victory garden is this: we dare not let ourselves off the hook too quickly. This vision was, after all, addressed to Christians who had a choice to make: step up to being faithful witnesses to Christ and suffer persecution, or duck out. They were being called upon to live with a solid trust in the Paschal Mystery even if it meant martyrdom. Sometimes we are called to be and to do more than we think we can.

I earlier mentioned my dog, Lizzie. Part of the nature of her breed, English Springer Spaniel, is that they are high-strung, high-energy animals. That I did not know when I bought her. After about ten days of chasing her around the yard, of trying to house-train her, and of being in the presence of such a nervous pet, I had had it. I told myself that I did not have either the time or endurance to work with her. So I called the breeder and asked if he would take her back. "I simply can't handle her," I said. His reply was not what I wanted to hear. "No, you can train her. It is easy." I wanted to be let off the hook. But if he had taken Lizzie back, I would have missed the fun of obedience class and of working with her, the personal challenge to become more patient and accepting, and, most of all, the pure pleasure of her love and companionship.

To be frank, this attitude of opting out is too much a part of the personality of the church. We let ourselves off the hook by telling ourselves we do not have the members, the money, the energy, the whatever to dream big dreams and to do big things. So, the refrain is: oh we can't do that. And we sing it over and over again. What might happen, I wonder, if we assumed that the Risen Lord would provide all that we need for us to be part of his choir, his mission, his adventure of faith? What might happen if we trusted in the ability of the Risen Lord to do great things with ordinary people? What might happen if we trusted that the money, the talent, the energy, and the people are available? If we did, Christ would use us to plant his garden. It would grow and develop. And on that great day, by ways and means we cannot fathom, the vision will blossom into the full reality of the victory of the One on the throne and the Lamb. We will be there in God's new Eden, singing with all the angels and archangels, all the saints and martyrs, and all those who have been marked with the cross of Christ forever:

> Christ Jesus, who though he was in the form of God,
> did not regard equality with God
> as something to be exploited,
> but emptied himself, taking the form of a slave,
> being born in human likeness.

> And being found in human form,
> he humbled himself
> and became obedient to the point of death—even death
> on a cross.

> Therefore God also highly exalted him
> and gave him the name
> that is above every name,
> so that at the name of Jesus
> every knee should bend,
> in heaven and on earth and under the earth,
> and every tongue should confess that Jesus Christ is Lord,
> to the glory of God the Father. (Phil. 2:5–11)

Questions to Help You Digest John's Vision

1. John's vision was written to and for churches in crisis. What crises does the church today face?

2. The vision of the garden in the new Eden is rooted in the reality of Christ's resurrection. The new creation will transform all time and space. What in your life and in your church stands in need of radical transformation?

3. What spiritual practices help make this vision an integral part of your mind and imagination?

4. What is your vision for a church transformed by the resurrection?

Some Thoughts at the End of the Trip

At the beginning of our time together, I recalled a childhood railroad trip with my sister and grandparents. Even then I was a fan of all things railroad, and that time spent on an actual luxury passenger train is still permanently impressed on my mind. I recall returning home, getting off the train, and simply standing and looking around. I saw the station, the platform, and the cars, the train personnel in a new and more vivid way as a result of that journey. As I reach the end of this journey of exploration about living in the resurrection, I pause and look around. There appear before me some basic factors that seem more vivid and important after this trip, and I want to lay them before you for your consideration.

First, we need always and everywhere to lift up Jesus Christ the Risen One. We need to proclaim clearing the Paschal Mystery as the good news of transformation. Because of the resurrection we can live in the bright sunlight and warmth of Easter. As we worship we have reminders of this resurrectional focus. Most of our churches have as a visual focus an empty cross, a symbol that points to Jesus who died, but is not on a cross or in a tomb. More importantly, we celebrate the Holy Eucharist, which is a time of banqueting together with our Risen Lord.

With all good intentions, however, we get off the track again and again. As persons, we always find it hard to take the focus off self and to put it on Jesus. And as church we get caught up in the latest programs about congregational growth, spirituality, various and sundry theologies, and a variety of other topics. Don't misunderstand me. We need to focus on ourselves enough to be aware of what is happening on the inside of our lives, and programs and theologies can spark some good developments. But they are all ancillary to the Risen Christ.

For instance, I often talk with people about the mission of the church and the ministry of all baptized persons. In the midst of a recent phone conversation about these topics, a thought shot through my mind. Whose mission? Ministry to what end? And why would anyone want to be involved in mission and ministry? Of course, it is Christ's mission, and we are involved in ministry to reproduce his ministry. But more importantly I cannot imagine why we would bother with any of this apart from Jesus and his resurrection. I realized that even ministry and mission, as important as they are, are secondary to the Risen Lord Jesus Christ. Our life is always about lifting up Jesus Christ.

Second, I am convinced that the church needs to be passionate about preaching and teaching the basics of the faith. I have an acquaintance who tells about greeting a long-time member after Sunday worship, and the man asked, "What is this resurrection you were talking about?" That is a sobering story, is it not? I have noticed that much of the preaching and teaching I hear focuses on calls for Christians to be involved in making the world better. And who would argue that our world does not need a lot of help? But the appeal for more involvement makes sense only in light of Jesus and his resurrection, otherwise the preaching and teaching are merely moralistic urging for nice people to be nicer.

Third, I was reading a passage from 1 Peter recently as part of Morning Prayer, and this verse seemed to leap off the page: "Beloved, I urge you as aliens and exiles to abstain from the desires of the flesh that wage war against the soul" (1 Pet. 2:11). Christians are called to be aliens and exiles. Today we are a minority voice in our culture, and the forces of influence in our society do not advocate the gospel. The church today is not the respected establishment of sixty years ago. We have a unique gospel to proclaim and a unique lifestyle to advocate. I believe we would be best served if we began to see ourselves as aliens in a culture that is not inclined to understand or accept us. In other words, we are again in the situation of the first disciples in the months following the resurrection. We need to return to the future by adopting the early church's mindset as ours.

I hope you have found this book both challenging and comforting. But above all, I hope it has been resurrectional for you.

Alleluia. Christ is risen.

The Lord is risen indeed. Alleluia.